ARCHITECTURAL DESIGN

EDITORIAL OFFICES:
42 LEINSTER GARDENS, LONDON W2 3AN
TEL: 071-402 2141 FAX: 071-723 9540

HOUSE EDITOR: Maggie Toy GUEST EDITOR: Richard Economakis EDITORIAL TEAM: Nicola Hodges, Philippa Vice, Rachel Bean, Ramona Khambatta
SENIOR DESIGNER: Andrea Bettella
DESIGN CO-ORDINATOR: Mario Bettella
DESIGN TEAM: Gregory Mills, Jason Rigby
SUBSCRIPTIONS MANAGER: Mira Joka

CONSULTANTS: Catherine Cooke, Terry Farrell, Kenneth Frampton, Charles Jencks, Heinrich Klotz, Leon Krier, Robert Maxwell, Demetri Porphyrios, Kenneth Powell, Colin Rowe, Derek Walker

SUBSCRIPTION OFFICES:
UK: VCH PUBLISHERS (UK) LTD
8 WELLINGTON COURT, WELLINGTON STREET
CAMBRIDGE CB1 1HZ UK

USA: VCH PUBLISHERS INC
SUITE 909, 220 EAST 23RD STREET
NEW YORK, NY 10010 USA

ALL OTHER COUNTRIES:
VCH VERLAGSGESELLSCHAFT MBH
BOSCHSTRASSE 12, POSTFACH 101161
D-6940 WEINHEIM GERMANY

CONTENTS

Peter Cook, Way Out West, Berlin

Richard England, Papal Stand, Ta'Qali, Malta

Ketterwell, Yorkshire
(Photo by Timothy Soar)

D1286666

Peter COOK
SIX CONVERSATIONS

I am holding six conversations with myself,
or six preoccupations which carry on over
time and around which I find myself working.
They don't run chronologically and I don't
become obsessed by one preoccupation only
to abandon it totally. It comes back again and
again and is layered into the others. Something that interested me ten years ago is still
there in the recesses of my mind and will
return in some aspect of a new piece of work.
Even to separate them here is very artificial.

CONVERSATION 1
MODESTY, FUN AND THE
ELLIPTICAL ENGLISH METHOD

Not a *direct* method, you will note, but an
elliptical method. Which is an ironic preoccupation, since I spend so much of my time in
countries (Germany, the USA, Israel) where
directness and definitiveness are honoured.
This is paralleled in my relationship with
architectural friends, which rarely consists of
a head-on discussion of positions or icons. It
is elliptical – considering a number of positions and *possibilities* and retaining the right
to harden up the definitions at the least likely
moment; the right to scramble the sets of
values; the right to introduce totally non-
architectural anecdotes; the right to hold an
ambiguous position that is not necessarily
disclosed, but perhaps unearthed by one's
friends, bit by bit. English phenomena,
particularly those that are found in parks and
gardens, fit the attitude perfectly. In the
picture of a little wooden seat under a tree
there is nothing apparently grand or heroic. It
is quite modest, certainly small and not
expensive. But look more closely at it,
imagine its likely context and its degree of
finesse. Almost certainly it faces a prospect
of several hundred metres and was commissioned by someone with power and influence. Beware of its apparent modesty: in the
same way, beware of the apparent modesty
and shyness of the English conversation . . .
the layers conceal an arrogance of assurance
and that the values can be shrugged at
suggests anything but weakness.
Arcadia A, 1975 (Detail)

IV

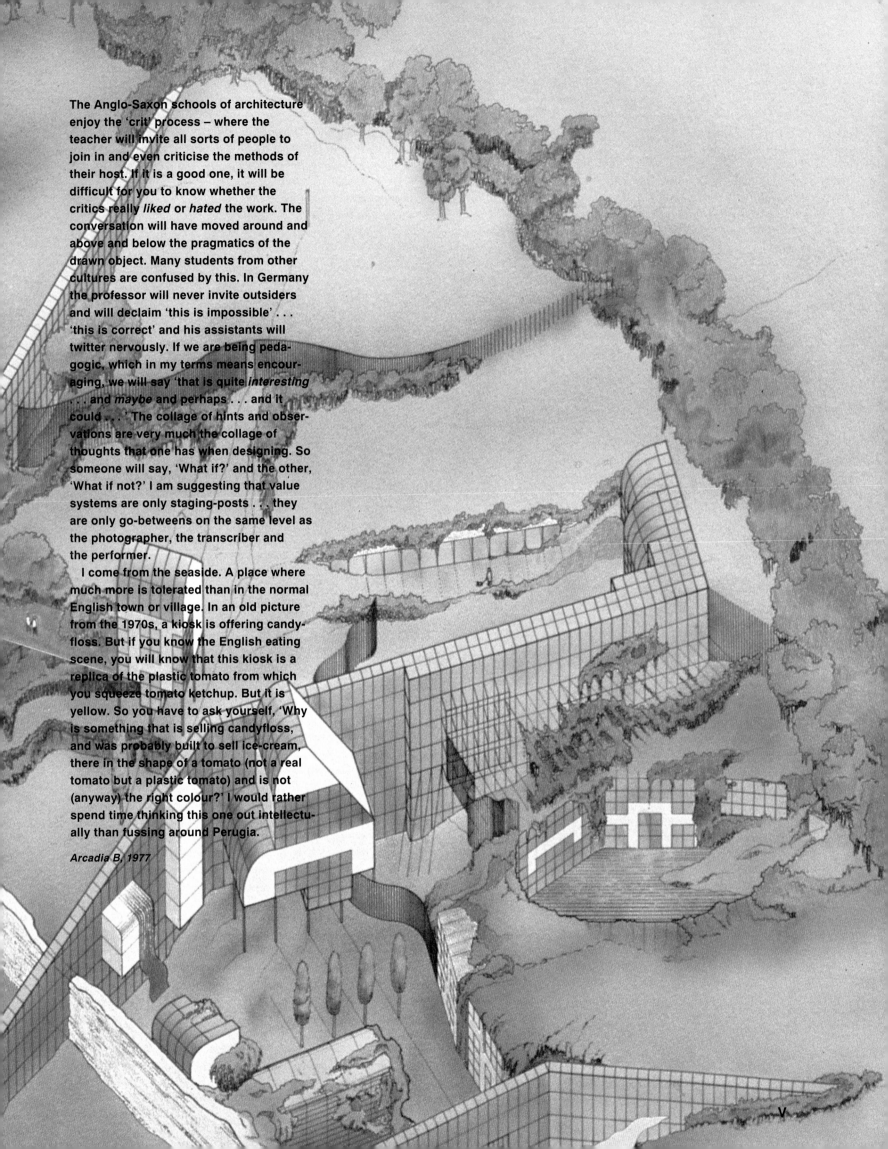

The Anglo-Saxon schools of architecture enjoy the 'crit' process – where the teacher will invite all sorts of people to join in and even criticise the methods of their host. If it is a good one, it will be difficult for you to know whether the critics really *liked* or *hated* the work. The conversation will have moved around and above and below the pragmatics of the drawn object. Many students from other cultures are confused by this. In Germany the professor will never invite outsiders and will declaim 'this is impossible' . . . 'this is correct' and his assistants will twitter nervously. If we are being peda-gogic, which in my terms means encour-aging, we will say 'that is quite *interesting* . . . and *maybe* and perhaps . . . and it could . . .' The collage of hints and obser-vations are very much the collage of thoughts that one has when designing. So someone will say, 'What if?' and the other, 'What if not?' I am suggesting that value systems are only staging-posts . . . they are only go-betweens on the same level as the photographer, the transcriber and the performer.

   I come from the seaside. A place where much more is tolerated than in the normal English town or village. In an old picture from the 1970s, a kiosk is offering candy-floss. But if you know the English eating scene, you will know that this kiosk is a replica of the plastic tomato from which you squeeze tomato ketchup. But it is yellow. So you have to ask yourself, 'Why is something that is selling candyfloss, and was probably built to sell ice-cream, there in the shape of a tomato (not a real tomato but a plastic tomato) and is not (anyway) the right colour?' I would rather spend time thinking this one out intellectu-ally than fussing around Perugia.

Arcadia B, 1977

V

The 'House in the Clouds' at Thorpeness is a
similar case. The house part is in a funny
place. In fact the house part is not a house
but was built as a water tank, and the part
underneath as the house. Except that this is
no longer true . . . for the community no
longer needed the tank and they came in with
the oxyaceteline burners and put a house
back into the tank. Sort it out in your mind,
this is a culture that is desperate to redis-
cover values and criteria in architecture!
I like things of this ilk and was therefore
quite ready to respond when the Leo Castelli
Gallery had its 'Follies' show. The 'Lantern
from Secret Blue' is almost certainly near to
the sea, and located a short distance from
the house and almost certainly viewable from
the terrace. 'How lovely, a sweet little white
tower,' murmurs the weekend visitor. 'I'm
sure you get a marvellous view of the sea.'
But if the visitor can be persuaded to walk
down to the tower, into the tower and climb
slowly up to experience the total surround of
blue – a strong Klein-like blue – and clutch
onto the evermore eccentric profile of the
handrail, he (or she) will of course emerge
and, yes, have a perfect view of the sea. The
spookiness of the inside against the bland-
ness of the outside has to be read against
the issues of assumption and discovery,
obviousness and actuality . . . I can't stand
the full frontal approach to architecture,
which is why I found Post-Modernism
such a yawn.

*Real City, Frankfurt, Skyglade, Westhafen, 1986
(reworked as Kawasaki Information Museum)*

Right back in the early Archigram days, the notion was that the existing vocabulary of architecture was a product of the philosophies of Buckminster Fuller or Paolozzi, so it is little wonder that when one is making architectural compositions they are composite as well as composed . . . both slurped and straight . . . OM Ungers meeting tomato ketchup at least halfway.

So both arrogance and modesty exist together in the English method; when making fun one is at one's most serious and the elliptical method enables the condition to be constantly moving . . . constantly under scrutiny. Even if my use of the word 'elliptical' is consciously borrowed from John Hejduk. You have to notice that the elliptical curve is one in which the speed increases and then decreases imperceptibly.

This text is extracted from the forthcoming Architectural Design Monograph 'Peter Cook: Six Conversations' published by Academy Editions, London, 1993, PB £19.95 HB £27.50

Real City, Frankfurt

RUSKIN AND TUSCANY

Following the success of the *Ruskin and Tuscany* exhibition at the Accademia Italiana in London, this spectacular collection of works by Ruskin and his followers, organised by Janet Barnes, Keeper of the Ruskin Gallery in Sheffield, is now being staged in Sheffield. The exhibition is unique as for the first time, the cultural relationship between Sheffield and Tuscany is being celebrated. The northern industrial city of Sheffield and the rich historical region of Tuscany may appear to have very little in common. However, there is a strong connection and it was made over a century ago by Ruskin himself, intent on asserting the humanity of arts as a common European heritage.

In 1875 Ruskin founded a museum in Sheffield which was designed to be an active and lasting centre of cultural influence. Initially named the St George's Museum, it played an integral part in the work of The Guild of St George which Ruskin founded in 1871 and which today is sponsoring the present exhibition. The Museum included a diverse collection of materials from medieval manuscripts to minerals which would encourage the direct development of personal sensibilities and the understanding of works of arts through close and detailed study.

Ruskin's interests covered a kaleidoscope of subjects. In his lifetime, through his prolific writings, teachings and lectures on history, social issues and art, he made a profound impact upon public taste in mid-Victorian England. As an art critic he was the champion of the then rather unpopular JMW Turner and, of course, the Pre-Raphaelite Brotherhood. As an artist Ruskin nurtured passionate interests in a variety of subject matters, including the art and architecture of the Italian Renaissance.

In this exhibition the focus is upon Tuscany and the impact its culture had upon Ruskin. Around 270 exhibits by Ruskin and his followers cover the field of paintings, sketches, daguerreotypes and books as well as diaries and other historical materials concerning Italy, which give us a privileged insight into the mind and thinking of John Ruskin. Ruskin visited Tuscany seven times over a period of 42 years from 1840, concentrating on the four major cities of Florence, Lucca, Pisa and Siena. Traditionally, Ruskin has been associated with Venice, the Alps and French cathedral towns. For the first time we have the opportunity to appreciate the importance of Tuscany which to Ruskin was the basis for modern European culture: a meeting place of north and south European; Greek and Gothic; and Christian and pagan cultures.

Ruskin's paintings and drawings are perhaps best known for their attention to detail. That is what initially attracted him to the Pre-Raphaelite Brotherhood who turned their back on all post-Raphael art, focusing instead on the minute and intricate detailing of the Gothic age. In this exhibition every watercolour and sketch is a tribute to Ruskin's involvement with detailing. His works are like photographic images and indeed he was fascinated by the discovery of photography. His interest in capturing the precise truthfulness of either nature or a manmade object reached the point of obsession and this is clearly apparent, for example, in the watercolour of part of the facade of San Michele in Lucca (1845) where he wrote in his notebook, 'I have been up all over it and on the roof to examine it in detail'. On the 1846 visit with his parents to Tuscany, his father recorded, ' . . . he is drawing perpetually but . . . only fragments of everything from a cupola to a cartwheel'. This is typical of Ruskin who preferred to draw certain sections where full attention could be dedicated to the tiniest details rather than a panoramic landscape where detailing was forsaken for the sake of atmosphere.

Indeed, Ruskin taught his pupils to paint by issuing each of them with a piece of white cardboard which had a square cut out of the middle. Pupils were encouraged to hold this card up to the desired scene and paint only what they saw through the square, sacrificing everything beyond it. This vigorous training is evident in the works of pupils and followers such as Bunney, Rooke, Newman, Collingwood and Burne-Jones, whose love of detail and fidelity to true colour and light is a definite tribute to Ruskin's teaching.

Ruskin's passion for Tuscany as a rich cultural centre (he once wrote, 'My whole history of *Christian* architecture and painting begins with this Baptistery of Florence') and for the intricacies of truthful detailing are captured and combined in this exhibition to present a most beautiful tribute to one of the leading lights of 19th-century English culture and history.   *RK*

Henry Roderick Newman, Piazza del Duomo and East Face of Baptistery, Florence, Ruskin Gallery, Sheffield

Thomas Matthews Rooke, Three Tombs beside Santa Maria Novella, Florence, Ruskin Gallery, Sheffield

Opposite: John Ruskin, San Michele, Lucca, Part of the Facade with Details of Columns and Arches, Ashmolean Museum, Oxford

IMAGE AND REALITY
RECENT WORK BY RICHARD ENGLAND

In February an exhibition at the Building Centre, London, illustrated over 25 recent projects by the Maltese architect and designer, Richard England. Sketches and photographs served to reveal the architect's concern with producing built form expressions of a valid contemporary regionalism. A variety of schemes included those for residential buildings (Sandrina's House, Mgarr); tourism (Comino Island tourist village); hospitals; and religious buildings, such as the Girgenti Chapel, the Church of St Francis and the Chapel of St Andrew.

England was born on the island of Malta. After graduating in Architecture at the University of Malta, he continued his studies in Italy at the Milan Polytechnic and also worked in the studio of the Italian architect-designer Gio Ponti. He is also a sculptor, photographer, poet, painter and the author of several books. Having written extensively on the direction of modern architecture, he believes strongly that it must respond and unite with the natural features of the site: architecture, he feels, must listen to its 'voices'.

These voices are ancient in Malta. The island's megalithic temples that were built over four thousand years ago by the earliest inhabitants, pre-date Stonehenge and the great pyramids of Egypt. The vocabulary of these stones and their enclosed spaces is evoked early on in his career: for example, in the Church of St Joseph, Manikata and in Villa La Maltija, Naxxar, where simplicity results in a powerful and fluid sculptural effect.

Uncomplicated expression is evident in most of England's oeuvre. Like other architects of his generation, he was influenced by the Modern Movement. Imported forms and ideas coexist with local sources in his early regional architecture: the Church of St Joseph can be seen to reflect the influence of Le Corbusier's Villa Ronchamp, while its pure and subtle form is absorbed wholly into the rugged, scorched landscape of Malta. Universal to the island is the building material: a soft, cream-coloured limestone through which simple cubic buildings of cut stone first emerged. Not only is the indigenous material influential to the whole system of construction on the island, but it also produces a visual impression of unity and harmony that is important to England. Initiated by a deep respect for Maltese tradition and character, he sought to develop a regional language of architecture that would respond wholly and eloquently to contemporary needs. A sense of mystery and tranquility pervades many of his works – such as his Garden for Myriam, St Julians; and the Old People's Home, Santa Venera. Rows of slender arches recall the paintings of De Chirico, the Italian Metaphysical artist. Also influential to the architect was Italo Calvino's book *Invisible Cities*. The presence of arranged fragments of buildings, severed columns and symbolic objects in his recent tourist village, San Tumas, lend an ambiguous air to his architecture. Although recent projects have encouraged some critics to place him under the post-modernist umbrella, England does not consider himself of this ilk; although he does appreciate Post-Modernism for emphasising the relationship to history.

England has received various International Awards and has travelled, lectured and exhibited around the world. The exhibition revealed the variety of the architect's work presenting a diverse range of schemes in novel ways. England is concerned with the spiritual qualities of architecture and of the place. He was impressed by the architect Louis Kahn for whom these qualities were inherent in that which is 'silent'. Through England's exploration of traditional vernacular architecture, solid can be seen to predominate over void – hence the sculptural quality of these volumes. Thick walls enable buildings to protect the inhabitants from the scorching heat in the summer and allow the building to keep warm in the winter. This has not denied his architecture a fresh vocabulary and dialogue with its site. Effects of intense light are used in a painterly manner, but also colour: subtle and bold colour that is reminiscent of baroque church interiors and of the Mediterranean – brilliant blues, warm reds, pale shades of grey and pink enrich San Tumas. Also shown in the exhibition were civic improvements for the streets of Valletta, the Maltese Capital where Renzo Piano was recently commissioned to undertake a master plan and design a new entrance to the city. England has also just completed the insertion of the Central Bank of Malta into the fortifications of Valletta. Currently, he has nine new buildings under construction in the University of Malta.

ILS

San Tumas tourist village, Malta, 1991

Opposite: Church of St Joseph, Manikata, Malta, 1962

NEW DESIGNS

POLICE ACADEMY, NEW YORK

In November last year Mayor Dinkins of New York City announced that the collaborative team of Ellerbe Becket and Michael Fieldman and Partners had won the international competition to build a new police academy. The project is to be located in the South Bronx and is fully funded by the city of New York. Construction will begin in the spring of 1996 and the aim is to complete it in 1999.

Mayor Dinkins stated that New York is recognised globally for its 'diversity and brilliance of architecture'. He added that while public buildings built by the government should emphasise function, 'as well as prudence in the spending of taxpayer's dollars', public architecture should add to and complement the urban design environment. It is strongly believed that the Ellerbe Becket/Michael Fieldman and Partners chosen venture will satisfy this criteria.

The team's competition-winning design is of transparent glass and steel volumes organised along two principal axes which frame extensive outdoor fitness and training areas. These two axes were designed in relation to the fundamental components of police training: mind and body. An eight-storey, 250 foot long administration block curves into a six-storey, 400 foot long academic block (hence, the mind) and within the curves of these forms, lies the physical education block, muster decks and outdoor fitness areas (the body), all positioned to take advantage of the south-east solar orientation.

The finished product will be a fine piece of architectural design with function, practicality and the surrounding environment all having been sensitively taken into account.

JERUSALEM SUPREME COURT

Officially opened in November 1992, the Supreme Court of Jerusalem was donated to the nation by Yad Hanadiv, the former Rothschild Foundation.

In 1984, the late Mrs James de Rothschild wrote to Shimon Peres, proposing the idea of a permanent home for the Supreme Court. In 1986, a two-stage architectural competition was held and an Israeli brother and sister team, Ram Karmi and Ada Karmi Melamede were chosen as the winners. The Supreme Court, built of stone in fortress style, occupies the central focus of the National Precinct in West Jerusalem. At present the precinct stands alone on its barren ground. Geometry one ascends a grand staircase similar to the Jerusalem stone alley, towards a curved glass curtain wall where a panoramic view of the city beneath is revealed. The space below the pyramid beyond is reminiscent of Absalom's tomb, a testimony to the centrality of law throughout time.

The Judges' chambers and courtyard are formed by two parallel sections surrounded by a stone wall with the Judges' chambers on the first floor, assuming a suitably respectful spatial presence of their own. The courtyard is made exclusively of stone and is bisected by a narrow channel of water on the central axis. The architects believe that this courtyard with 'the stone quarried from the earth and the water reflecting the sky juxtapose the biblical symbols of truth and justice'.

The building is typical of the architecture of Jerusalem with its forboding walled-in scheme revealing strong religious and spiritual overtones only on entry.

BERLIN GREEN SCHEME

A scheme by Louisa Hutton and Matthias Sauerbruch (LHMS Architects) has won the competition to design an extension for the 16-storey 1950s office tower headquarters of the housing society, Gemeinnützige Siedlungs- und Wohnungsbaugesell-schaft Berlin mbH (GSW).

The development at Kochstrasse, Kreusberg, Berlin, is one of the first post-unification proposals for the historic centre.

Building costs are estimated at £37 million and work is due to commence in autumn 1993, with Ove Arup and Partners as the consulting engineers. The brief called for a new structure, providing an extra gross floor area for offices and shops. The winning scheme responded with 'Green Architecture' that reflects the architects' desire to challenge the use of conventional technology and resources.

The scheme employs a second glass skin to form a solar flue which acts as a thermal buffer in cold weather. The updraft rate of air increases and decreases within the solar flue in proportion to the changing climates. It is an energy-saving building, one of the first of such structures to be built in Europe.

The intention is to continue the post-war attitude of green, open spaces for the Kreuzberg district by offering two publicly accessible green squares, whilst respecting the existing 18th-century street grid-plan.

LHMS Architects is a London-based, Anglo-German partnership founded in 1988. Through success in a number of competitions, the partnership has already achieved a high design profile. Their work has been exhibited in London, Berlin and Zurich.
© Coralie Langston Jones.

SHELTER

Sensitive to the threat of natural disasters, Future Systems have designed a low-cost, large span, collapsible tent-like structure for use in such an event. This 'universal shelter' is conveniently adaptable, serving as an emergency shelter for up to 200 people or as a storage facility, a clinic or a distribution centre for food and medicine.

Using lightweight PVC coated polyester material it is in addition collapsible for ease of transport and can be erected by unskilled people in very little time. When packaged, it is reduced to one item, hence ensuring easy and uncomplicated transportation.

The Shelter is built along the same basic lines as a collapsible umbrella and only 12 people are needed to erect this structure by each simply taking one of the 12 ribs and pulling it into the locking position. There are 12 anchorage points which can take a variety of different loads catering for wind speeds of up to 130km/h.

Future Systems have also shown environmental concern in the design of the Shelter. The white outer surface of the membrane reflects up to 80% of solar radiation achieving an internal temperature reduction under the most extreme conditions of 12°C more than is achievable with a canvas tent. In contrast, the impregnated metal particles on the inner surface emit little radiant energy, reflecting heat back into the enclosure to provide warmth at night. Cross-ventilation is achieved by allowing air to pass into the enclosure at a low level through the perimeter skirt and to exit at high and mid levels via the central hub and flap details.

Architectural Design Special Profile

INTERVENTIONS
IN HISTORIC CENTRES

THE BUILDINGS OF MAGDALEN COLLEGE

The question of how to build in historic city centres has inspired the architectural profession over the last twenty years. Architecture has reached what is arguably the most critical crossroads of the century. Architects around the world have begun to break out of the long period of self-imposed abstinence from contextual considerations, seeking ways by which to engage traditional and historic settings in meaningful dialogue and producing some of most engaging proposals in recent times. Differences abound, however, and raise questions concerning the exact nature of intervention. How far should historical precedents be taken as models? How are contemporary social and technological parameters incorporated in the new proposals? How should tradition and originality be understood? How can we retain traditional urban forms within the constraints of contemporary practice? What is the nature of the dialogue between architects and the people for whom they build?

One project which tackles all these questions is that of the development of Magdalen College where an Academy International Forum was held in October 1992. Much of the debate revolved around the scheme by Demetri **Porphyrios** for the college and he was there to explain many of the delights within the design. Other valuable contributions to the discussion include those by Maurice **Culot**, Rob **Krier**, Sir Philip **Dowson**, Robert **Adam**, Terry **Farrell** and John **Simpson**.

£14.95
ISBN: 1 85490 199 0 Paperback
305 x 252mm, 96 pages, extensively illustrated
Publication date: June 1993

ACADEMY EDITIONS • LONDON
42 Leinster Gardens, London W2 3AN Tel: 071 402 2141

THE BRITISH LIBRARY

Over 40 years ago, in 1951, in the early years of the newly founded Welfare State, the government made the decision to build a British Library as a magnificent centre of culture to reflect the wealth of scholarly talent this country has embraced over the centuries. The British Library would be a home to the nation's collections of books and literary material, housing it all under one roof.

The plan was then abandoned until 1972, when the government created an Act of Parliament to build the library. Unfortunately, problems have plagued the building of the library and today it seems to be facing an increasingly gloomy future. Completion and opening has provisionally been set for 1994 and 1996. To many, even this seems too optimistic.

Colin St John Wilson was chosen to design the British Library which, if completed, will surely add to the country's cultural heritage. His original plan was approved, but in 1980 it was discarded, construction began and what we see today of the building and the plans for the completed structure is radically different. The government came to the firm conclusion that it was not going to continue providing all the funds that the original plan demanded. Hence, the design had to be forsaken and sacrifices had to be made: the Oriental manuscripts, the catalogue hall, the printed books reading room and thousands of reading room seats were abandoned.

Nevertheless, Wilson was determined to design an alternative and inspirational building that would be worthy of such a centre. The plan was revised accordingly and what we see today is a vast building which is slowly rising from the ground of two brick stretches which converge together on the Euston Road where they form a plaza. Some critics insist that the combination of the striking red brick and the stainless steel of the window grills and eaves is too harsh. However, Wilson who is comfortable in the knowledge that the image will mellow with time, is unperturbed by such comments.

The designs for the interior of the library are impressive. On entering the building the visitor will certainly feel overawed by the soaring quality of the architecture with one end completely devoted, from floor to ceiling, to the collection of leather and gold spined books from King George III's library.

Besides the King's Library, there will be a variety of reading rooms and a further 12 million books will be stored in four levels in the basement. Throughout the building there will be sophisticated air-conditioning with a filtration system to ensure optimum preservation.

Through the years funds have been given sporadically with the result that building has taken place at a painfully slow pace. The budget has passed £450 million and some critics are commenting that the library is in fact too small and too late.

Britain deserves a library of suberb quality to house its unique collection of literary items. However, all this will only take place if the government continues to support the building financially.

NEW WAVE JAPANESE ACHITECTURE

KISHO KUROKAWA

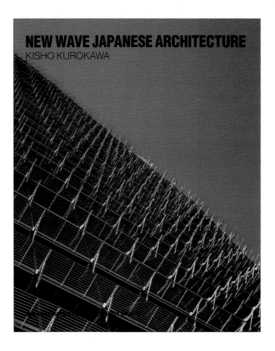

This book is the most up-to-date illustrated account of current developments in Japanese architecture. It has been compiled by Kisho Kurokawa, himself an internationally celebrated architect , whose penetrating and thoughtful essay guides us towards understanding the innovative and exciting new projects which feature in this book. In addition, Kurokawa helps us to understand current projects against the background of Japan's distinctive and sometimes exclusive cultural and spiritual tradition.

Thirty of Japan's most vigorous contemporary architects – among them Itsuko Hasegawa, Kazuyo Sejima, Yasufumi Kijima, Tadao Ando and Kan Izue – have been selected. Two projects by each are examined complete with drawings and plans. Short accompanying texts by the respective architects explain each design and the philosophy behind it as well as more technical information. Kurokawa also points out that these architects support a variety of architectural traditions yet share a common heritage: even the most seemingly high-tech Japanese building has its roots in an invisible spiritual tradition.

New Wave Japanese Architecture not only enhances our understanding of Japan's development as the world's most technologically advanced nation, it also gives us a glimpse of buildings which will influence future generations worldwide. This book gives us a new vision of Japan as it moves towards the 21st century.

420 pages, over 850 illustrations, mostly in colour
ISBN: 1 85490 157 5 Hardback £49.50

ACADEMY EDITIONS • LONDON
42 Leinster Gardens, London W2 3AN Tel: 071 402 2141

THE BUILDINGS OF LONDON ZOO

by Peter Guillery, RCHME, 1993, 146pp, b/w ills, PB £12.95

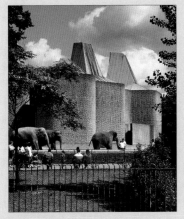

London Zoo is one of the nation's most loved institutions, an established tradition which has provided entertainment and education to all age groups for nearly 170 years. In 1991, when the Zoological Society announced that closure seemed inevitable due to financial conditions, public response was tremendous. Donations flooded in and the threat of closure seemed to ebb. At present, the decision hangs in the balance, tempered by the government's 1992 decision to grant the zoo £10 million along with a company called 'Zoo Operations Ltd' which holds responsibility for managing the zoo with a view to improving its future.

When the decision to close the zoo was first announced, the Royal Commission on the Historic Monuments of England decided to carry out a survey on the zoo's architecture. The RCHME felt the need to draw public attention to these buildings as the zoo has some quite exceptional architecture, with many of its buildings standing out in areas of innovation. *The Buildings of London Zoo* is the result of the survey undertaken by the Royal Commission and it focuses on the great variety of buildings, devoting 146 pages to, amongst other elements, their history, their original qualities, the reasoning behind the requirements of each building and the innovative qualities.

London Zoo opened its gates to the public on its present site in Regent's Park in 1826. It has been an important vehicle for reflecting the trends in architecture and also, the use of technological developments in industrial materials. Furthermore, the need to house the animals in an environment akin to their natural habitats in the wild has increased over this century, initially influenced by Carl Hagenbeck, a German, who spoke at length in the late-19th century about introducing nature into the lives of caged animals.

In 1913-14, the Mappin Terrace (named after the donor) was built, designed by Sir Peter Chalmers Mitchell. It is the largest feature in the zoo with a radius of 87 metres and was the first animal environment in Britain to answer Hagenbeck's call. The Mappin Terrace is an outdoor reinforced concrete building consisting of a three-tiered quadrant topped by a mass of artificial hills. Each tier is separated by public circulation paths which lead the viewer from one enclosure to the next, each enclosure independently housing deer, goats and bears. Construction is not only suitable but practical as well. For example, within the artificial hills of the goat enclosure lie chambers, held up by an intricate trellis system of reinforced concrete beams, which house water-tanks for, and high-level louvred air discharge vents from the nearby Aquarium.

Even earlier in its history, in 1849, the zoo responded to technological advances by building the very first Reptile House in the world. Each glass cage within the building had its own landscaped background with thermostatically controlled heating systems. The reptiles had the privilege of ultraviolet light – a rare luxury in those early days of electricity.

Another architectural area in which the zoo is seen to have covered new ground is in its zoomorphic buildings. The Elephant and Rhino Pavilion is probably the best example, designed by Sir Hugh Casson and Neville Conder and Partners in 1962-65, which replaced the original 'Swiss chalet' style building. Once again, the pavilion is built of reinforced concrete, with vertical rilling and a hand-hacked finish to create the rough textured look of the skins of both elephants and rhinos. This is not only entertaining and playful but functional as well.

Not all the buildings, however, have been designed with the Hagenbeckian principle in mind. In some cases the natural personalities of the more exuberant animals have been allowed to dominate the design of the architecture. The most appropriate example of this is the Penguin Pool, one of the greatest attractions of the zoo. Penguins provide tremendous entertainment with their antics and in 1934 when a new pool was being designed by Berthold Lubetkin and Lindsey Drake, it was decided that the playful nature of the birds should be emphasised. The Penguin Pool is a fine example of early modernist 'Constructive' design, the entire building is constructed (once again) from reinforced concrete in an elliptical shape with interlocking, cantilevered ramps of varying thicknesses which provide the penguins with a suitable stage. To the north of the pool is a nesting box and to the south, away from the nesting, is a diving tank. This is walled with plate glass at our eye level to provide good viewing as the penguins swim about with astonishing grace.

The late-20th century has seen buildings of skilled engineering. The African (formerly Eastern) Aviary was originally built in 1827, then a new building was erected on the same site in 1863 and now it has been largely remodelled with a spectacular addition of outdoor caging. This work was carried out by the architectural practice of John Bonnington Partnership and the structural engineers Whitby and Bird. Once again, London Zoo has been seen to be leading the way in implementing technological developments as it is the first wire aviary in Britain. The cage is constructed of a tall hooped tubular-steel frame with parallel wires stretched across the arches of the upper part of the frame. They are then anchored at either end to fans on a wing-like steel footing with immense concrete foundations. However, the caging is practically invisible as each wire, made of stainless steel alloy developed from North Sea structures, is only 0.09mm in diameter. There are 1,688 wires in all which run the length of 30 metres at 31mm intervals.

Without the zoo a wealth of diverse and fascinating buildings which can only exist successfully within a zoo environment, will be lost forever.

EXHIBITIONS

THE FRANK LLOYD WRIGHT GALLERY

In 1934 Frank Lloyd Wright first met the Kaufmann family, at a time when his professional position was very unstable. Wright was 67 years old and had built practically nothing for the previous decade. The Kaufmann's contributed immeasurably to the revival of Wright's career by supporting him through commissions for buildings and donations to the Taliesin Fellowship.

The Victoria & Albert Museum are now the proud owners of a complete office, including the walls, floor, ceiling, furniture and textiles built by Wright for Edgar J Kaufmann. The room, which was Kaufmann's private office in his Pittsburg department store, is the centrepiece of a new gallery dedicated to the architect. It is the only gallery in Europe devoted to Frank Lloyd Wright and the most comprehensive collection of his work outside the United States.

The chairs, stools, desk and cabinets which were used by Kaufmann everyday from 1938 to 1955 survive intact as does the striking mural relief in swamp cypress wood and the upholstery and carpets designed by Wright and woven by the celebrated weaver, Lois Saarinen.

Alongside this complete work, other examples of Wright's output are on display, including furniture, prints, books and graphic designs.

The gallery has been funded by a generous donation from Mr Paul Mayén, a New York architect and interior designer, and friend of the late Edgar Kaufmann Jr. Additional funding was provided by the Alexander T & Tillie S Speyer Foundation and the Newhouse Foundation.

BEFORE AND AFTER PLANNING

An exhibition earlier this year at the RIBA concentrated on a very interesting aspect of architecture – the effect of the planning process on building design. The exhibition displayed 15 projects in a 'before and after' state to illustrate how buildings are enhanced or, conversely, distorted by the planning process. Amongst the schemes on display were competition winning projects, a small rural house in Scotland, a large commercial retail scheme in the south of England, schemes planned for sensitive historic sites and a major urban development.

TADAO ANDO

Ando entered the architectural world in the early 1970s, startling it with his sharp criticism of contemporary culture with its focus on functional convenience and comfort. Ando believes (and has shown) that architecture in today's society is distracted by economic, legal and technological concerns. Hence, it is built too conservatively, sacrificing the human spirit altogether. Turning his back on all this he examined the true relationship of architecture and man, architecture and nature and man and nature, offering new ideas capable of awakening human sensibilities.

Initially Ando concentrated on private houses and commercial buildings but then in the 1980s, he expanded into churches, public cultural facilities, schools and museums. Recently he has directed his visions abroad and was the architect responsible for the Japan Pavilion at Seville's Expo '92; the Art Institute of Chicago's Japan Gallery and FABRICA (the Benetton Research Centre) in Italy amongst a number of others.

Ando's work has taken the architectural world by storm, turning all conventionally industrial ideas on their heads. His beliefs gathered power through the 1980s and they are currently becoming a campaign of international dimensions as we approach the 21st century.

The exhibition in Paris, which is in character a record of Ando's crusade against existing architectural concepts will be travelling later in the year to London and Barcelona. Tadao Ando Exhibition, Centres Georges Pompidou, Paris, 3 March-24 May 1993.

ART EXCHANGE BETWEEN RUSSIA AND THE WEST

Possibly the most exciting development in the world of art this decade, 'From the Treasuries of Eurasia' and the 'George Ortiz Collection' signify an unprecedented cultural exchange between the former Soviet Union and the West. In 1988, George Ortiz visited the USSR and began negotiations with the Ministry of Culture, proposing the idea of lending his extraordinary collection of 40 years to the country, in exchange for the opportunity to personally choose a number of works of art from Soviet museums, which would then go on show in the West.

The idea was agreed to and Ortiz made his selection on aesthetic grounds choosing works which he believed would do justice to the wealth and breadth of ancient culture throughout the USSR. The cultural diversity of the Eurasians inhabiting the area around the Black Sea is the focus of 'From the Treasuries of Eurasia', with specific emphasis on the regions encompassing the Urartu Empire, whose descendents reached as far east as Siberia and who were close relations of the Greeks.

This exhibition embraces a collection of some 170 items from 15 institutions representing 18 different cultures. The objects range from the Stone Age to the Byzantine and also include a number of spectacular Tsarist acquisitions, private donations and confiscations from outside the Soviet Union.

George Ortiz's personal collection of antiquities with over 300 masterpieces from a collection of over one thousand works of art spanning 30 cultures from the Neolithic age to the late Byzantine period, started its tour in St Petersburg in February. Previously, individual works have been loaned to important exhibitions worldwide but this is the first time the public can marvel at the sheer quality of works in this collection. The collection includes such works as an alabaster figure of a Sumerian bull-man from Umma dating from the 3rd millennium BC (the only other known alabaster figurine of this period is in the Iraq Museum, Baghdad) and a wooden figure of a Nukuoro deity from the Caroline Islands. Visitors to this exhibition will be treated to an extraordinary evocation of man's early artistic endeavours. 'From the Treasuries of Eurasia' and the 'George Ortiz Collection' are rarities in themselves and every effort must be made to see both. 'From the Treasuries of Eurasia' will travel from the Kunsthaus, Zurich, to the Museum of Kyoto, Japan, where it will be on show from 6 June-4 July 1993.

The 'George Ortiz Collection', which started its long journey at The State Hermitage Museum in St Petersburg will be on show at The State Pushkin Museum of Fine Arts in Moscow from 6 May-27 June 1993, and then at the NY Carlsberg Glyptotek in Copenhagen (dates to be confirmed). The exhibition will be travelling to London and Japan as well; however, exact locations and dates are yet to be confirmed.

For further information, please contact: Sue Bond at Sue Bond Public Relations, Tel: (071) 381 1324.

LILIAN COOPER

The Galerie Amsterdam recently held an exhibition on three graphic artists who graduated from the Gerrit Rietveld Academy in June 1992. One of the three was Lilian Cooper whose motivation for work this year has been the influence of a series of standing stones in Northern Scotland. Her paintings aim to show the integral nature of these stones with their ability to dominate over the flat, barren landscape whilst harmonising with the environment at the same time. Cooper was initially attracted to the stones for their 'forlorn isolation', for their simple shapes and the fact that although man had placed them there, nature had made them part of herself.

Cooper's works are not impressionistic, they are not immediately recognisable as standing stones. Instead, the images seem to crawl out of the canvas, with frenetic lines drawing us into the large, encompassing forms. The approach is representational with the final result being an emotional response to what Cooper sees in her mind's eye. Her year of experimenting and exploring has led towards an independent and evocative analysis of what has become a very personal interpretation.

TOYS THAT TEACH

'Toys that Teach' at the Canadian Centre for Architecture, Montreal, was the third successive annual exhibition which centred around its collection of over 300 architectural toys and games, spanning nearly two centuries of toy manufacture in Europe and America. Collected by the New York sculptor and architect Norman Brosterman, the toys were bequeathed to the Centre in 1990.

The architectural toy typically looks to the world of 'real' buildings, reproducing columns, arches and windows in miniature form. In the early 19th century, sawn wood blocks were used to create such toys with the result in the 20th century of the invention of toys like Lego. How-

ever, there is another class of toys inspired not by human objects but by the elementary forms of geometry found in nature: cubes and spheres, cones and cylinders, rods and prisms. No other architectural toys have as rich a variety of uses – these toys serve not only for building but also for mathematical exercises, drawing instructions and even lessons in coordinating and movement.

The collection represents the full range of construction toys from the 19th century to present day. This includes sets of paper architecture, traditional wood building blocks, construction kits of artificial stone, miniature villages which reflect early, simple, vernacular construction methods and toys that incorporate the use of modern materials such as iron and steel that were widely used before the introduction of plastic by the toy industry in the 1940s.

Among the most influential of 19th-century toys were the geometric blocks used in the early kindergartens established by the great German educator, Friedrich Fröbel (1782-1852) and his followers. While studying mineralogy in Berlin, Fröbel became convinced that the geometric principles found in crystals permeate all of nature, forming what he termed 'the fundamental unity of the universe'. Living in a period which mutually embraced German Romanticism and the Enlightenment, Fröbel united wide-ranging ideas about pedagogy, geometry and the natural world in his kindergarten curriculum, believing this would appeal most strongly to the natural instincts of children. The programme emphasised creativity, physical dexterity and social interaction. These toys were named Gaben or 'gifts' and were presented to the child in a precise sequence of increasing complexity, beginning in the nursery and continuing until the age of seven.

Fröbel's legacy of combining simplicity with intricacy was probably best exemplified in Kennedy's Dissecting Mathematical Blocks of 1893, a prominent exhibit at the CCA exhibition. When the leather strap is removed, on the sphere for example, the ostensibly solid wooden block breaks apart into a number of segments. Furthermore, each of the segments can then be unfolded into even smaller wedges, each intricately hinged, finally revealing the sphere to be a composite of 48

separate polygonal shapes.

Breaking the sphere down and then putting it together again is a physical task that most children would enjoy and benefit from more than studying a similar exercise theoretically on a blackboard or a piece of paper.

Fröbel's ideas found rapid recognition in the United States and during the second-half of the 19th century, most American pre-school education was based on the Fröbel system. At the same time many 19th-century geometric toys reflect how extremely he influenced his contemporaries and how these ideas filtered into the 20th century.

'TWIN TOWNS' MOSAIC MURAL

Officially opened by the Burgermeister of Reutlingen on 19 October 1992, this impressively large (16m x 2.6m) mosaic mural is a public tribute to the European twinning ideal and a celebration of German-British friendship. The people of Reutlingen, near Stuttgart, in Germany generously commissioned the mosaic mural as a gift to the people of Ellesmere Port, their twin town. It is also a gift from a British private developer in whose shopping centre the mosaic resides.

Susan Goldblatt and Magnus Irvin were chosen to create this mosaic which was pieced together from thousands of vitreous coloured glass mosaic tiles. Goldblatt, an architect-artist is a graduate of both Liverpool University of Architecture and the Byam Shaw School of Art. Irvin is a fellow member of the Barbican Arts Group and has created murals and mosaics in public locations throughout England.

The mosaic portrays the combined traditional icons, horizons and

buildings of the twinned towns in an interesting two-dimensional, geometric manner. This does not detract from the historicism of the buildings of Reutlingen or the more industrial nature of the buildings of Ellesmere Port but rather, reflects the art and architecture of an old medieval town and the rather severe lines of the newer industrial town respectively. In the centre of the mural is the medieval walled City of Reutlingen with its striking gated towers and hills beyond. The waters from Reutlingen's surrounding moat are seen flowing into Ellesmere Port's canals and coastal waters. The industrial and naval architecture at the approaches to Ellesmere Port and Helsby Hill are echoes of the medieval gated towers at the entrances to Reutlingen. The outstanding iconography, decorative features, buildings and roofs of the twinned towns are juxtaposed at several levels to form a visual and colourful confluence. By layering images of the two towns, the complex and different cultures are given a multiple shared perspective. The union of the two is emphasised by the inclusion of the EC flag amongst the coats of arms. From inception to completion the mosaic took two-and-a-half years to create with a team of eight requiring five months to construct and erect the work.

An Apology
In the Architectural Design, 1-2/90 issue, we published three essays under the heading Architecture: A Place for Women. These essays were titled 'Room at the Top? Sexism and the Star System in Architecture' by Denise Scott Brown, 'Educating for the Future' by Matilda McQuaid and 'The Studio Experience: Differences for Women Students' by Anne Vytlacil. We neglected to indicate that these essays came from a book entitled Architecture: A Place for Women, which was published by the Smithsonian Institution Press in 1989. Ellen Perry Berkeley, a senior editor with The Architectural Forum and Architecture Plus, is the book's editor; Matilda McQuaid is the associate editor. Denise Scott Brown owns the copyright of her essay. The other two essays are copyrighted by the Smithsonian Institution Press. We regret our oversight in failing to give full details at the time we republished this interesting material.

BOOKS

SAVE THE JUBILEE HALL by Chuck Anderson with Ray Green, Random Thoughts, London, 1992, 207pp, b/w ills, HB price N/A

Ray Green, the Chairman of the Jubilee Market Traders, provides an interesting and thought provoking account of the battle to preserve Covent Garden and Jubilee Hall following the relocation of the wholesale fruit and vegetable market.

An area which is now one of London's most popular tourist and shopping centres could easily have ended up as another large mono-functional office development. Instead, through the dedicated campaigning of market traders and the local community, the buildings around Inigo Jones' Covent Garden Piazza remain. The Edwardian Jubilee Hall and a modern addition house a modest amount of office space, a new community sports hall, restaurants, workrooms and fair-rent housing for 28 families over a market hall where 400 traders earn their living.

Ray Green discusses the political, financial and practical battles which resulted in one of London's most popular and famous multi-use inner-city developments.

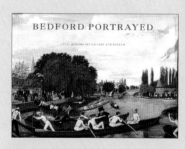

BEDFORD PORTRAYED Preface by Halina Graham, Introduction by Richard Wildman, Commentary by Min Dinning, Cecil Higgins Art Gallery and Museum, 1992, 88pp, b/w and colour ills, HB price N/A

18th and 19th-century topographical drawings and prints of Bedford from the Museum's collection are placed next to modern day photographs to show the continuity and change of Bedford's townscape. These, along with the informative text, provide interesting reading for those with an acquaintance with the area.

TRANSITION No 38 Special Issue by Robin Boyd, RMIT (Royal Melbourne Institute of Technology), 1992, 300pp, b/w ills, PB AUS $35

This special celebratory issue commemorating more than a decade of the magazine is devoted to the architect Robin Boyd.

More than an architect, Boyd devoted much time to all the arts, appearing in all the media as well as adult education programmes and he wrote regularly for the press wanting his ideas to be accessible to all. Some of his peers and friends included Walter Gropius and Kenzo Tange.

This issue prints essays from the 1989 conference focusing on all the areas Boyd covered from projects from tall buildings to chair design. With many previously unpublished works appearing for the first time it is more than a mere history of the man but a collection of important fragments which have wider implications for Australian architecture.

With many images, photographs, cartoons and letters this is a lively and important work for this post-war period in Australia and the world.

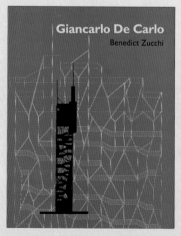

GIANCARLO DE CARLO by Benedict Zucchi, Butterworth Heinemann, Oxford, 1992, 228pp, b/w and colour ills, HB £40

This book traces the ideas and influences of De Carlo's work, a leading figure of the Italian architectural scene.

From his rise in the 40s and 50s – preceding the Post-Modernists by a few decades – with attacks on the International Style, this book traces De Carlo's undermining of the old Modernist establishment to his involvement in town development in Urbino in the 1950s.

With an essay by De Carlo as well as a wide-ranging interview and excerpts from his writings, often for the first time translated into English, this book gives a unique insight into this important architect and thinker.

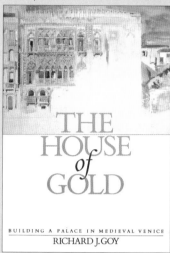

THE HOUSE OF GOLD Building a Palace in Medieval Venice by Richard J Goy, Cambridge University Press, 1993, 304pp, colour ills, HB £60

Famous the world over, this book tells the history of the construction of Cà d'Oro ('House of Gold') on the Grand Canal in Venice.

With a general introduction to the city of Venice at the beginning of the *quattrocento*, Dr Goy discusses the background that led to the building of the house with the marriage of two Venetian families.

With general writing on the building industry in this period as well as detailed recreations of the practical aspect – from laying bricks to terrazzo and the magnificent facade – Goy creates a vivid impression of the 20 years devoted to the erection of the house and analyses the relationship of its creator: Marin Contarini with his craftsmen and the private role of Contarini himself. He concludes by discussing the architectural importance of the palace and its historic legacy.

Excellent textural detail and images exist throughout this scholarly work giving us an informative and lively insight into the workings of 15th-century craftsmen. With beautiful, detailed photographs, this is an essential text for those interested in the art and architecture of Venice and its many public buildings.

BOOKS

BOOKS RECEIVED:

EMERGING VISIONS OF THE AESTHETIC PROCESS, PSYCHOLOGY, SEMIOLOGY AND PHILOSOPHY *edited by Gerald Cupchik and Janos Laszlo, Cambridge University Press, Cambridge, 1992, 331pp, b/w ills, HB £35*

URBAN DESIGN: *Street and Square by Cliff Moughtin, Butterworth Heinemann, Oxford, 1992, 224pp, b/w ills, HB £29.50*

JOURNAL OF HEALTHCARE DESIGN *Vol IV, National Symposium on Healthcare Design Inc, 250pp, b/w, $75*

FROM IDEA TO BUILDING – ISSUES IN ARCHITECTURE *by Michael Brawne, Butterworth Heinemann, Oxford, 1992, 233pp, b/w ills, PB £19.95*

DESIGNING FOR PUPILS WITH SPECIAL NEEDS – Special Schools, Department for Education, Architects and Building Branch, *Building Bulletin 77, HMSO, London, 1992, 88pp, b/w ills, PB £14.95*

EMERGENCY LIGHTING – For Industrial, Commercial and Residential Premises by *Stanley Lyons, Butterworth Heinemann, Oxford, 1992, 177pp, b/w ills, HB £25*

JAPAN DESIGN – DESIGN OF THE FUTURE by *Matthias Dietz and Michael Mönninger, Taschen, Cologne, 1992, 176pp, colour ills, PB £9.95*

TÜRME ALLER ZEITEN ALLER KULTUREN by *Erwin Heinle and Fritz Leonhardt, DVA, Stuttgart, 1992, 343pp, colour ills, HB £35*

TOWARDS AN ECO-CITY: Calming the Traffic by *David Engwicht, Enviro book, Oxford, 1992, 192pp, b/w ills, PB £9.99*

FRANK LLOYD WRIGHT'S HOLLYHOCK HOUSE by *Donald Hoffmann, Dover Publications, New York, 1992, 118pp, b/w ills, PB £10.95*

ARCHITECTURAL EDUCATION Issues in Educational Practice and Policy by Necdet Teymur, ?uestion Press, London, 1992, 112pp, HB £14.95 PB £7.95
As Director of the CIAS (Centre for International Architectural Studies at the School of Architecture, University of Manchester) Teymur is in a prime-position to know and question important architectural issues.

What wider visions must architecture embrace? What new, what long term and what practical objectives must educators set themselves? And last, though by no means least, can a deeply flawed educational system be reformed by tinkering with mechanics of course structures or the number of years that students study?

These are among a few of the questions raised in this much needed and timely book which examines a number of curricular and policy issues. The need for postgraduate courses and alternative modes of research, the role of theory in design teaching and exchange in international global education are all reviewed. It assesses the implications of the latest Governmental interference from an educational point of view.

This book is necessary reading for anyone interested and concerned for the future of state architectural education in Britain, Europe and the World in today's political climate.

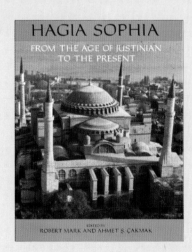

HAGIA SOPHIA From the Age of Justinian to the Present edited by Robert Mark and Ahmet S Çakmak, Cambridge University Press, 1992, 255pp, b/w ills, HB £55
This book examines the form and structure related to one of the masterpieces of world architecture that has intrigued architects, engineers

and historians for centuries.

Included in this academic and questioning book are many essays organised along themes that include structural precursors, observations of the fabric of the Byzantine Hagia Sophia and related buildings, structural studies of the Byzantine building and the Ottoman Hagia Sophia and its influence on contemporary architecture.

This great building begs answers to questions that the authors discuss, for example the capacity of the present structure to withstand a major earthquake.

Historical background, physical environment, design and the state of the Hagia Sophia building over time are all included and crystallised by detailed elevations and photographs. This book provides an invaluable source of close reference and inspiration.

ART DECO ARCHITECTURE: Design, Decoration and Detail from the Twenties and Thirties by Patricia Bayer, Harry N Abrams, New York, 1992, 224pp, b/w and colour ills, HB $49.50
In a lavishly illustrated study, Patricia Bayer explores the diverse forms of Art Deco architectural design and its distinct, sometimes regional variations. The style's origins in the Arts and Crafts Movement, *fin-de-siècle* Vienna, Cubism and the Bauhaus are traced. The wide variety of building types to which it was applied are examined, ranging from the Chrysler and the Empire State buildings, the 'cathedrals of commerce' which have come to epitomise Art Deco, to private residences, restaurants, theatres, cinemas and monuments. And in a chapter entitled 'Revivals and Replicas', Bayer discusses how Post-Modernism has borrowed from its repertoire of motifs and idioms to produce what, in some cases amounts to a full-fledged revival.

SINAN: Ottoman Architecture and its Values Today by Godfrey Goodwin, Saqi Books, London, 1993, 136pp, b/w ills, HB £35.00
Godfrey Goodwin analyses the work of one of the greatest 16th-century architects, Sinan Abdulmennan, and discusses how he revolutionised inherited Ottoman building methods. The Ottoman tradition was one based on structure. To this Sinan brought an awareness of the psychology of space, and by breaking down the distinct forms that had created a certain rigidity, he freed both interior space and interior form.

The book contains thorough comparative studies of Sinan's major buildings, the most important being the mosque of Salim II at Edirne. To complement this Godwin examines Sinan's underlying architectural concepts based on the mathematical theories and concepts of ancient Greece, and shows how these paralleled the intellectual revolution in the West, embodied by such men as Bramante and Palladio.

STOCKHOLM TOWN HALL by Elias Cornell, Byggforlaget, Stockholm, 1992, 143pp, b/w ills, HB price N/A
With an informative text illustrated by luxurious photographs, many of which are in colour, this book tells of the construction and plans for Stockholm's Town Hall in the late 19th to mid-20th century.

Ragnar Ostberg, who designed the Town Hall, was one of Sweden's leading architects of this century. His work embraced strands of Art Nouveau mixed with a particular blend of northern and southern Swedish elements.

The book follows the progression of the building work and the ideas involved in the creation of this important civic and cultural centre.

ARCHITECTURE IN ARCADIA

WILLY HARBINSON, PERCY THOMAS PARTNERSHIP, LUCCOMBE HOUSING

Architectural Design

ARCHITECTURE IN ARCADIA

OPPOSITE: DAVID LIGARE, VIEW OF LEON KRIER'S PLINY'S VILLA PROJECT; *ABOVE*: PIERRE BARBE, DOMAINE DES
TREILLES, MAISON *BARJEANTANE*

ACADEMY EDITIONS • LONDON

Acknowledgements

All material is courtesy of the architects unless otherwise stated.
The basis for this magazine was the International Symposium and Forum *Architecture in Arcadia: Development and the Countryside*
which took place on 21 March 1992 at the Royal Academy of Arts. This event was organised by Andreas Papadakis and MaryAnne Stevens
in conjunction with Clive Aslet the editor of *Country Life*.
Giles Worsley's article *Rural Housing Design: The Search for the Middle Way* was first delivered as a speech to the
Royal Town Planning Institute Annual Conference on June 7, 1990.
The EC Green Paper on the Urban Environment was first published by the Commission of the European
Communities in 1990.
Edwin Venn *aerial perspective of Poundbury*, Front Cover; pp46-47
Jordi Fontanals Modelmaking *model of Belvedere Village*, pp52-53

Photographic Credits
p12 George Oldham *View of Cotswold village; pp20, 36* A&B Photography *16th-century barn conversion;*
pp20, 34 Timothy Soar *Housing at Luccombe; p28* Rural Development Commission, Graham Sapsford
Ketterwell, Yorkshire; p35 Bob Seymour *New house at Horseheath; p86* Photography Dominique Delaunay/
Institut Français d'Architecture, Paris; *pp3, 89-93* Dominique Delaunay *Domaine des Treilles, Maison
Barjeantane; Can Gerxo and Sa Païssa de'n Casetes*

CONSULTANTS: Catherine Cooke, Terry Farrell, Kenneth Frampton, Charles Jencks
Heinrich Klotz, Leon Krier, Robert Maxwell, Demetri Porphyrios, Kenneth Powell, Colin Rowe, Derek Walker

HOUSE EDITOR: Maggie Toy GUEST EDITOR: Richard Economakis
EDITORIAL TEAM: Nicola Hodges, Rachel Bean, Philippa Vice, Ramona Khambatta
SENIOR DESIGNER: Andrea Bettella DESIGN CO-ORDINATOR: Mario Bettella DESIGN TEAM: Gregory Mills, Jason Rigby
SUBSCRIPTIONS MANAGER: Mira Joka

First published in Great Britain in 1993 by *Architectural Design* an imprint of
ACADEMY GROUP LTD, 42 LEINSTER GARDENS, LONDON W2 3AN
ERNST & SOHN, HOHENZOLLERNDAMM 170, D-1000 BERLIN 31
Members of the VCH Publishing Group
ISBN: 1-85490-196-6 (UK)

Contents

ARCHITECTURAL DESIGN PROFILE No 103
ARCHITECTURE IN ARCADIA

RICHARD ECONOMAKIS
BUILDING ARCADIA

The traditional European habitat is characterised by an underlying respect for the countryside; but today the accelerated growth of the industrial metropolis threatens to destroy the precious balance that has existed for millennia between the built and natural environments. Modern zoning laws and an explosion of indiscriminate speculative planning have precipitated a dangerous reduction in the amount of productive land.

Renewed interest in traditional modes of expression in architecture has concurred with and helped to bolster the pre-industrial attitudes towards the countryside, while 'tolerating' suburbia in as much as it is a mendable, though undesirable product of zoning practice. A new generation of European architects and planners has reasserted an urbanism that preserves the age-old respect for the integrity of the countryside, stressing density and a concentration of functions in the city. Like a tree or boulder, the city is thus seen again to occupy a specific, limited place in nature. Leon Krier's proposal for Poundbury has provided a model for a stream of proposals and executed work, François Spoerry's Gassin in France and the Rue de Laeken in Brussels perhaps best exemplifying the new European outlook. Demetri Porphyrios' Belvedere Village develops these ideas in a more rural form.

Though hailed as a principle commodity of the new 20th-century industrial market economies, the modern suburban house offers its occupants the psychological benefits of green open space while placing them at the periphery of towns in an unproductive relationship to both the idea of *civitas* and countryside. Large-scale developments, argue the new traditionalists, can only be justified if they are conceived in connection with an urban centre which offers a mix of functions and local occupational incentives – otherwise they will remain a primary cause of commuter wastage in time, energy and space. Proximity to a truly urban environment is therefore essential, and called for more and more by a public that has grown disaffected with the idea of commuting.

The use of a classical or traditional vocabulary for the suburban house can be justified as appropriate both on historical and planning grounds. The modern house, after all, is a relative of the Villa or Country House, which brought a civic style to the countryside as a way of stressing the owner's urbanity. In any case, if the new proposals to urbanise the suburbs hold sway, then it would be fair to say, too, that the classical language (so long as it relates to the regional historical and cultural context and makes competent use of the load-bearing tectonic science out of which it has grown) is appropriate as it lends itself readily to the notion of a traditional *res publica*. The readiness of new traditionalists to design in a classical manner, as evidenced in the work displayed in this issue, exemplifies the new attitude which seeks to surgically transform the bedroom community into a contained neighbourhood no longer expanding haphazardly but in respect and deference to the countryside.

The confusion surrounding the calls for an integration of traditional urban and architectural attitudes (summarised in the oft-asked question 'why a traditional and not a modernistic or a 'contemporary' aesthetic, even within the context of a traditional plan?'), is only natural, as it goes to the root sources of contemporary cultural angst, questioning the formal legitimacy of both new traditionalism and high-tech modernism. It would no doubt be difficult to imagine most of the projects illustrated in the context of this discussion about the countryside as informed by anything other than the specific regional vernacular or historical styles, which they are unanimous in adopting. The regional types, it should not be forgotten, developed out of tectonic and programmatic considerations particular to an area and its economy. Timber, stone, brick and other naturally available materials are found in abundance depending on climate and geography, and it makes perfect sense to use them rather than imported industrial products. High-tech modernism is an architecture that evolved specifically within the economic and social sphere of the modern industrial metropolis, and takes a categorically anti-regionalist attitude towards building in the countryside, proposing, instead, a transposition of high-tech vocabulary and materials when a new building is erected for whatever purpose – thereby upsetting, through its provocative rejection of perfectly adaptable and well-tested materials and typologies, the very *genius loci* that has sustained and expressed communities for centuries. In the specific case of modern suburbia, a superficial, nostalgic rendering of traditional architectural forms has been sanctioned as a propitious offering to the restless, and potentially explosive collective subconscious which seeks more and more to pick up the strands of cultural continuity abandoned by a world obsessed with the vision of a high-tech *terra nova*. It is against these fantasies that the collected built and projected work in this publication have pitched themselves.

CLIVE ASLET

SECRETS OF THE GODDESS CERES' CROWN

The countryside is Britain's most popular leisure destination. Fantasy game players are among the most novel of a whole throng of recent arrivals, from jet-skiers to hot air balloonists, whose advent coincides with a period of unprecedented uncertainty for farming.

During last year's Royal Show, the Royal Agricultural Society of England announced that it had received planning permission to build a £17 million Museum of Food and Farming – claimed to be the first of its kind in the world – at its show ground at Stoneleigh, in Warwickshire. Nothing could better exemplify farming's reluctant entry into the heritage business. Farmers have always been custodians of the landscapes they created; now some of them must make a virtue of that custodianship to augment falling incomes.

Inevitably the landscape is *changing;* it always has changed. Land taken out of production under the 'set aside' scheme looks scrubby and uncared-for. Meanwhile, by an unfathomable EC paradox, other land is forced to yield not less, but more – or to produce different things. The effect can be haunting. Parts of Kent have been given added charm by the veils of blue netting now used to protect vineyards. Elsewhere, the intensification of agriculture diminishes the experience of visiting the countryside. Until recently, the best crop farmers could grow seemed to be houses – a very different matter from changes due to agriculture alone. Changes in farming practice can be reversed; even hedgerows can be replanted. Land that has been put under bricks and mortar or tarmac is unlikely ever to be reclaimed.

In total, fewer houses were built in the 1980s than in other decades since the Second World War. But in many areas of the countryside their impact was greater, because of the relaxation of the planning controls that had so well preserved rural England for years. Previously, open farmland was protected against building by the priority given to food production. When this economic and strategic justification disappeared, the countryside found itself protected only by sentiment. Sentiment cannot often hold its own against the powerful commercial interests promoting development.

Housing estates sprouted on the edge of villages. In some areas planners insisted that an approximation of vernacular materials was used. Nevertheless, the planning of these estates had little in common with the traditional forms of the villages to which they were attached. Developers claimed that there was an over-whelming need for more houses. Then came the recession and house prices fell. Suddenly there was not so much talk of the desperate necessity for these homes.

There is one benefit arising from the present recession: it provides a breathing space after the hectic pace of the let-rip 1980s. But only, perhaps, for the moment. The pressures that caused so much damage in the last decade – over-development and suburbanisation – have been suppressed, but they have not gone away. They are ready to erupt as soon as prosperity returns. Two months ago, a survey by Mintel International revealed that two thirds of all adults in Britain would choose to live in the countryside if they were able. Hardly surprising, given the state of British cities. But what will the countryside be like when the aspiring country dwellers finally reach it? Indeed, will they be able to reach it, or will they merely find themselves in another traffic jam?

Fortunately change can be for the better as well as for the worse. Landscapes that have become impoverished over centuries can, it is hoped, be reclaimed, allowing wildlife and spontaneous beauty to return. Agricultural buildings need not be unsympathetic to their surroundings. In the Lake District, the National Trust is constructing barns, adapted to the demands of today's larger machinery, which are wholly in keeping with the vernacular farmsteads to which they are attached.

Neither the countryside nor the city is an island. City dwellers need the countryside both for food and spiritual refreshment, while the countryside needs the money for the produce it sells to cities. This, as Demetri Porphyrios observed in the Symposium, was symbolised in the Classical world by the accoutrements of the goddess of harvest, Ceres. She wore a walled city in her crown to express this vital interdependence. Building over the countryside, depriving future generations of the chance to enjoy its bounty, would not have seemed civilised behaviour to the Ancients; it belonged to an earlier phase of human development: nomadic pastoralism.

Whatever the state of agriculture, Britain must not revert to this barbaric attitude towards the land. Britain has not been as successful at preserving the harmony of its cities as many of its neighbours in Europe. But in the protection of its countryside it has been unsurpassed. We cannot afford to take it for granted. This issue of *AD* is intended to stimulate thought among architects – whose thinking is too often city-based – before the next on-rush of development takes place.

ARCHITECTURE IN ARCADIA

Academy International Forum: The Royal Academy of Arts, London. Saturday 21st March 1992. The International Forum on *Architecture in Arcadia*

Paul Finch: This afternoon's subject could scarcely be more topical. The question of our attitude to development in the country has exercised increasingly the minds of environmental politicians, pressure groups and the general public in many different ways. As far as design is concerned we have just had the announcement of the Planning Policy Guidance Note Three, which gives a coherent account of the last Government's attitude to how we should be designing in the country. Development, from now on, should be sustainable. By 'sustainable', Michael Heseltine does not mean self-supporting new towns full of autarchic houses; he means re-using urban land. There are some interesting statistics which show that a large portion of land, for example for housing development in urban areas, has been used two or three times prior to any current incarnation.

Paul Finch

There are elements of contradiction in any government's attitude to the countryside; for example, the belief that the country should be protected from development on the one hand, and yet on the other hand that there should be fiscal and planning encouragement for the development of golf courses and the conversion of manor houses into what used to be called the 19th hole. In popular culture we see, for example in a soap opera like *The Archers*, these great arguments being played out. There the rich businessman, a farmer, Brian Aldrige, a model of the high-tech agriculturalist, suddenly discovers the joys of investment in venison and swimming pools and leisure pursuits, while dear old Pat and Tony are down the road making organic yoghurt and debating whether to supply the local department store with their very naturalised cream. On a more public level there is the great argument about hunting in which we see the last kick of the town/country argument.

Of course these arguments aren't simply about the country, but about something much deeper. In the background there is a continuing 'sub theme' to the town and country: is the town a parasite on the country sucking in the food, sucking in the wealth created and sucking in the population? Or is it the other way round? Is the country a parasite on the city? Does the country suck out money being created in productive enterprise? Does it suck out taxes from Britain and from Europe so that farmers can waste everybody's money growing things that nobody wants to eat? Well, I hope some of these things will be explored this afternoon and I'm going to ask Clive Aslet, who has organised this afternoon's event, to begin.

Clive Aslet

Clive Aslet: Thank you. The first thing I have to say about this town-versus-country debate is that, in terms of the press coverage architecture gets, the town wins by a mile. Nearly all press comment is about urban projects. The 1980s saw an absolute explosion of housing estates, leisure facilities, developments around motor ways, super stores, theme parks and so on. The great majority of that was never discussed at all in the architectural press or in the newspapers, so I'm very pleased to have a symposium which is going to discuss the quality of architecture and other kinds of built development in the countryside. I think it is an extremely neglected subject and one which is very important and very central in British thinking, or should be.

The International Architecture Forum

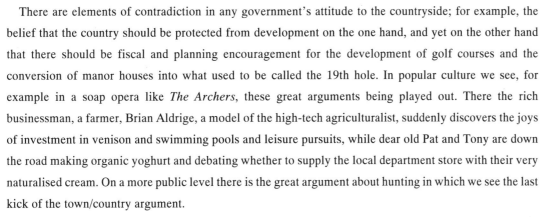

Robert Adam

Robert Adam, New House on Country Estate near Basingstoke, Hampshire

The background to this debate is obviously that now there is regarded to be a surplus of agricultural land since, as we all know, we appear to be producing too much food (though Britain is in fact a net importer of food). But is this only a present surplus of land? Is it possible that, in the future, that land will be needed again? Land which has been built over is never going to be available again for any other kind of activity. Just as people who are living in recession can never see the possibility of boom years, so people living in the boom years can never see the possibility of recession. If you live in a period with an apparent surplus of land, it is difficult to see that in the future that land might be needed again. Nevertheless, I think that there is some point in thinking about it. For example, whatever you feel about climate change, that is obviously something that is going to affect land use considerably throughout Europe, because Britain is predicted to become one of the more productive areas if the change of climate takes place. There could be a great impulse towards using biomass fuel; fuel from crops that will have to be grown somehow – have to be grown on land. If that land has already been built over, there won't be any prospect of using it to grow fuel. Once land has been urbanised that is essentially the end of it from a productive alternative point of view.

So I would question whether we are wise to use what surplus land we appear to have for growing buildings, so to speak, and I would also suggest that the problems in the countryside don't lie in the development of the countryside for buildings but they really lie in the development of the cities. The challenge is to provide cities which can offer an attractive environment so that we won't have to go into the countryside. Future development is likely to be in terms of housing for single unit accommodation, for people who are leaving home early and the increased number of people who are divorcing or living to old age without a partner. Those people are much better accommodated in cities than they are in the countryside. I would like to see a moratorium on any kind of development in the countryside until we get these priorities sorted out.

Robert Adam: I sympathise that buildings in the country never get reported. I also suffer from the problem of getting architectural journalists to sit on trains and in cars for long enough to see my buildings.

I have just come up from the countryside for this discussion, which is paradoxically in the middle of London. I live in the country, or what is loosely called the country, and I have a slightly different tack from Clive since I believe that the idea of the countryside lies at the heart of the English. I use 'English' advisedly – at the heart of the English idea of itself. A magazine called *Country Living* has had a huge success. Whereas a magazine called *Metropolitan Living* has, I understand, folded. *Country Living* had a little fair a few weeks ago which they actually had to stop people coming to by making public announcements on the radio after the first half day. It was held in Islington!

I believe this whole idea of the countryside is at the core of the way British people see themselves. It goes right back, some people claim, to the 18th century, when the aristocratic group didn't have the sole preserve of the land. Real life in the country was often extremely nasty and extremely poor. So when you bought your bit of the country, you turned it into what you thought the country ought to be like: a pastoral landscape or model village. It is a countryside myth that we've operated on for centuries. These myths are very interesting. If you made your money in industry you bought a farm – preferably one of the forms of sporting farms – and that is still the case. One of the things that makes a farm worth money at the moment is to have a shoot on it. Nevertheless, the 'country ideal' is the ideal of a better past that never existed.

We have the misfortune of believing our own tourist guides. Scotland believes it is a land of health and heather, the French believe they are great lovers and the Italians believe they live in a hot country. That is why there is no decent heating in Italy. The English believe they live in a land of little cottages. I suffer from these myths, I also make money out of these myths, but they have had a very significant impact on development. One which I particularly loathe is that ubiquitous architectural style of the 'neo-vernacular'.

Those who know me know I hate it. It is a myth propagated through the planning system so suburban parodies are cottages but they are not, they are too big. So because of building regulations the housing estate is called a village and goes by the name 'Dingly Dell' or 'Broad Acre Lane'. Tescos have turned into huge barns, although they are nothing like barns because they are surrounded by cars, which barns are not. And office buildings become cottages that look like someone has pumped up with a bicycle pump.

Then there is the 'ideal village'. The real village has gone and what has destroyed it, interestingly enough, is what is called 'agri-industry', since the number of people working on the land has diminished quite dramatically. People get very worked up about a 'village shop'. Well, within living memory, villages didn't have one shop they had lots of shops. They had a baker's and cobbler's and all sorts of things. There wasn't just a village pub, most villages had lots of pubs. But the really important thing was that they had very poor people living there, which you don't get so much now. The other thing that has destroyed them is transport. Social equalisation makes people not so much upwardly mobile as outwardly mobile. The suburb was an ideal village, and now the village is a suburb largely created by transport.

Nostalgia is something that spawns strange ideas. One is that of 'no growth and no change'. Two villages I know now were twice the size a hundred years ago. But you are not allowed to make them grow, because someone decided that this ideal moment was actually round about 1950 and this is the time for no more growth. The other one is preserving hierarchy: ie, no more big houses. The trouble is there aren't any very poor people anymore, which makes this rather difficult. The other paradox, in my opinion, is that no change *is* change, because in fact change is something that has been taking place all the time since the beginning of villages and to stop change is actually a very dynamic process of change.

The idea has arisen that villages used to have local people in them, which of course they did. Firstly, the local people couldn't get out; secondly, there were particular jobs there for them; and finally they were dead poor, so that was the only place they could afford to live anyway. It is claimed that local people literally have a hereditary right to live in a village. But many of the folk who insist upon this hereditary right don't actually work in the villages, they just want to stay there because their parents lived there.

George Oldham

Ken Powell

Roger Scruton: In my view, two historical processes are threatening the English, Welsh and Scottish countryside: first, the habit of 'filling in' towns and villages, and the reluctance to begin real new towns, with the obligation that this will impose to think things through. (I mean, of course, new towns built to scale, in the traditional materials, with streets and lanes and churches.) Secondly, the migration to the country of suburban sentimentalists with no understanding of the natural world. (Damage done by these people can easily be witnessed in the campaign against fox-hunting, an activity that has been an integral part of rural life and *the* major force in conserving habitats.) It is possible to alter the first of those processes; I doubt that you could alter the second. I therefore propose dividing England into two areas: the one a theme-park for softies, governed from Westminster, with roads, parking-spaces, 'safari' areas full of badgers, foxes and generally cuddly vermin; the other (to which special passes will be required), governed from Taunton, for example, in which anyone will be allowed to live provided (a) he is not an architect, (b) he is carnivorous, and not adverse to allowing death into Arcadia (even if adverse to allowing architecture).

Paul Finch: Thank you. I wonder if it is true that the planning system encourages the ubiquitous neo-vernacular either in towns or in the countryside. I am going to ask George Oldham, as both a former Newcastle City Architect and also formerly chief architect of Barratt Homes, to make a comment.

George Oldham: For a brief spell I was the chief architect for a developer, but I parted from that developer because we couldn't really see eye-to-eye on a number of things. But if I might make a comment about

Maxwell Hutchinson

View of a Cotswold village

these politics of control which Clive Aslet appears to subscribe to very strongly: I do believe that they are in fact ruining both town and country. Robert Adam made all the proper points about no change being change and it is some 20 years now since Nan Fairbrother wrote *New Lives, New Landscapes* which was an extremely important book, certainly in developing the way I feel about the countryside. One thing is absolutely for certain and that is that we do live in a changing environment: trees die, trees need replacement, landscapes will change, they'll change for all kinds of reasons and so will our habitats. And the sort of political correctness about what is an urban or what is an Arcadian form, seems to me to be totally irrelevant. What is relevant is that we need in the order of two million houses before the year 2000, if we are to sustain any quality of life.

We must take positive decisions on how that might be approached. The sanctity of the greenbelt has for 40 years been a keystone of British planning policy, but while this has been largely successful in containing existing settlements, it now requires radical review. I'm very sad that Heseltine is now saying that the countryside has got barriers round it and feels that all development can take place in an urban situation. Fifty years ago Frank Lloyd Wright spoke at the RIBA and advocated pulling down whole sections of London so that the people of London could have some breathing space and some more parks and could establish 'Broad Acre' cities elsewhere. My idea is closer to Wright's than to this artificial restriction.

The last decade has seen an increasing incidence of the breakdown of the existing infrastructure in our cities, towns and villages as more houses are added to outdated roads and sewage systems. Towns and villages with balanced communities have been altered beyond recognition by over-development. Quality has been sacrificed for affordability with the inevitable rise of land prices as a result of planned land shortage.

What would it mean if we put two million houses in the countryside? Something like 55 per cent of development is actually on sites that have already been used. That leaves 45 per cent of the two million homes – say a million homes. Six million acres of farmland, as he said, will need to be taken out of production by the year 2000. If you put those million homes into the countryside they would consume less than one per cent of that farmed land. We are talking about a tiny impact in some senses, in terms of the overall Arcadian environment.

What we are missing, I believe, is a vision of what we could actually achieve. If I walk the Cotswolds I don't walk them actually to gain a great deal out of the landscape *per se*. It is the landscape plus the built environment of those villages in the Cotswolds. Why are we so fearful that we cannot create something of our own age which will not replicate in its built form, but replicate in energy and in fact even improve the environment that we find all over the place in despoiled industrial landscapes? I believe that this restriction is entirely antithetical to people's aspirations and to what we could actually produce as architects. The alternative is the creation of new village settlements beyond the greenbelt, each an identifiable community responding to the needs of the 21st century.

Maxwell Hutchinson: We should stop being so pompous and pious about the country and take our lead from Mrs Thatcher, who decided that we should build most of the two million homes we need to build during the course of this decade in the countryside. She called in the large house builders. They set up Consortium Development, and she charged them with going away and building most of these houses. They put forward proposals for new villages in the countryside including Foxley Wood, but when it came to the crucial moment for the Government to make a decision about the village, they could not do it; they turned it down and Consortium Development was wound up. When it comes to it we are afraid to bite the bullet.

I believe that we can and should develop the countryside vigorously. I cannot see how we could possibly cope with our future building needs without facing the challenges of developing the countryside. One of my disappointments with Richard Rogers' Labour Party manifesto for London is that it concentrates on the needs of the city without the reflexive need for developing the countryside. I share Robert Adam's view about the vernacular and the way in which planning guidance since the *Essex Design Guide* has told us that the only way to develop the countryside is in traditional architectural language, using what the planners call 'traditional materials'. I see plenty of good new buildings in the countryside. I can't positively conceive of how we can take this country forward to the end of the millennium without developing new schools, new health care facilities and new retirement facilities in the countryside.

As to the type of architecture – the style in which we build – I think we are over reverential. I have absolutely no doubt at all that the only way that we are going to have a balanced development in the United Kingdom between towns and the countryside is to challenge ourselves as designers by finding the appropriate mechanism to develop the countryside.

Christopher Day

Christopher Day: I'd like to pick up on the parasitic relationship between town and countryside. The fact is that our settlements have, historically speaking, condensed out of rural activity. Now, in the past it was possible to do this in an unthinking, habit-bound and inherently sensitive way. We've lost these activity connections and our new developments in the countryside have no relationship for the people who live there to the working development of the landscape in the way that our ancestors had. If we are to make developments which are in harmony with the place, we must find an entirely new, conscientious way of going about this. We can no longer do it out of habit and expect it to be any better than a bungalow estate.

Paul Finch: Can I bring you in here Demetri Porphyrios? Is it actually possible to produce successful buildings for the countryside, or is it simply a question of creating successful buildings full stop and their relationship to the countryside is really neither here nor there? They simply exist because they are needed.

Demetri Porphyrios

Demetri Porphyrios: Civilisation has always been linked with the city. This can be seen in terms like *civis, civilis, citizen* etc. The goddess of grain – the Greek Demeter and the Roman Ceres – is always represented wearing a crown, shaped in the form of a turreted city. I suppose this is a reference to the interdependence between agriculture and cities, between country life and city life both understood in a productive sense. The whole history of western civilisation has shown clearly that there can be no contradiction between countryside and city. In fact, the two have always grown together. Now let me just look at it from another point of view. We may recall the famous piety of Aeneas, who founded Western civilisation. When he left Troy, Aeneas carried two things: his father and the household gods, or *penates*. The *penates* were specifically the gods of harvest and of grain storage. I think we must not forget that as long as land remains unmanured or undeveloped it stays a savage wilderness and therefore it has no name. Land is named – that is, it becomes an object of language – only when it becomes civilised or when it is exploited in relation to the city. The ancients understood clearly that for land to exist, it must always be replenished. We moderns, however, have reverted to a nomadic exploitation of land which lays waste to it. Must modern industrial progress inevitably lead to a degraded landscape? Tradition has shown us that this need not be the case. But to develop the land it is important to follow a few simple guide lines.

Firstly, one should take a regional point of view. Rampant development with scattered mega-markets, housing, leisure and industrial parks linked with superfluous highways is not civilised exploitation of land but nomadic barbarism. We see this about 5.30 every day when the barbarians take off for the countryside.

Secondly, physical development should be concentrated as much as possible. Do not build here and then somewhere else. Build everything here until this *here* cannot sustain any further development. *Here* is a metaphor: the walled city surely is no longer a military requirement but can serve as the grand metaphor for

Lebbeus Woods, Underground Berlin

civilised settlement. If we are to survive as a species, and I assume we don't want to destroy ourselves like the dinosaurs, we must once again understand urbanisation not as sprawl but as densely built towns with the maximum of the countryside left open.

Thirdly, maximum use should be made of abandoned sites or derelict industrial space which exist in towns with a view to creating urban neighbourhoods which combine residential, leisure, commercial and workplace activities. There can be no short cuts. Urbanisation and the countryside are two sides of the same coin. I know it is not an easy goal to achieve. What is reassuring is that the EC Green Paper has adopted many of the principles some of us have been arguing for over the last 20 years. I have some of those extracts here: 'This new concept takes as its model the old traditional life of the European city'. These are documents of the EC which adopt theories we have been promoting for years. 'This new concept takes as its model the old city, the old traditional life of the European city, stressing density, multiple uses and social and cultural diversity.' Or, elsewhere: 'Concretely, this attitude may lead to three convergent orientations, avoiding strict zoning, defending architectural heritage and avoiding escaping the problems of the city that are created by the periphery', etc.

Paul Finch: Well, I am going to ask Leon Krier if he would like to add to that in a moment. But first can I turn to you, Lebbeus Woods, and ask you to make some response to the idea that, not only the recreation of the traditional European city will be ordained from Brussels as it were, but also that there will be the sort of perceptible regulations about how we should develop the countryside as well.

Lebbeus Woods: It strikes me that we are still stuck in a kind of linear way of thinking about this problem. A kind of idea of progress going on and on. What is the best step going to be? Do we develop or not?

The countryside will be developed for urban, suburban, exurban uses – of that there is no doubt. The crucial question is how? But what sort of society sponsors and then must live under the dictation of conventions, standards, norms which are issued from a bureaucratic centre, located in London, or perhaps Brussels? The answer to this has already been decided, and it is a unified society, an 'economic' community, justly named, but frightening in its implications for former fields in the hinterlands of England. The unified and self-levelling economic machinery will produce at best a homogenised landscape, cut according to patterns designed for a general case, embellished with enough local flourishes to satisfy the natives. And who will care – or notice – after all. The grand plan should work pretty well. Sadly, that is probably what will happen.

We are in a time which requires a lot of reassessment: what is our idea of nature? What is our idea of city? What is human? Are human beings natural? Is nature human? What are the links there?

Efficacy does not make an authentic experience. What is authentic, at least with regard to countryside, is what is not planned, what in fact *cannot* be planned. Aside from the so-called charm of bucolic surroundings, which are after all agricultural in origin, is the shock of the discovered, the wilderness of the natural, which is wild only because it is not controlled, roped-off or ghetto-ised. To preserve the countryside in its pure state, without building of any kind is a fine idea, and solves the problem of destroying its wildness, therefore also of interferences with appreciation of its naturalness. Paolo Soleri's *Arcologies* come to mind. And on a lesser scale, Calcutta, or – some suggest – Tokyo and London, though these cities offer no untrammelled countryside as contrast. They do prove that at present, or in the near future, humankind can be packed into super-dense ant-heaps, there to enjoy the wonders of their kind, assuming that they have or will develop the mentality of ants. But short of imprisoning earth's burgeoning human populations in over-crowded cities, the countryside probably cannot be spared from the messiness of human habitation.

Let's just argue over the next step. We've taken a qualitative leap towards the next century. In the 20th century, human thought and even the idea of human knowledge have undergone a tremendous revolution.

Leon Krier: I find the pretensions of modernism are most difficult to digest. It is not the results so much but the pretension about this fantastic qualitative leap. This has happened probably in nuclear physics but it hasn't happened in architecture. In fact, there has been a qualitative leap in the wrong direction.

Arcadia has developed nowhere else like it has in England. In Europe the relationship with the countryside is quite different. I always wondered, coming to England first, why people were sitting eating their picnic out of the back of their car on busy country roads or in depressing car-parks next to a country house. They even maintain these habits when they go to Europe because they don't know that there is a different relationship to the countryside there. The countryside there is actually common, even if it is privately owned. The fact is that you can't get to the countryside if you live in England unless you own a very large piece of land but even that is too small. Even a large piece of land does not represent the countryside. It is an indescribable luxury to have grown up in a country, such as Luxembourg, where you can cycle out for a picnic along a river.

Leon Krier

As Demetri described, every Friday and Saturday afternoon you have the barbarians exiting from the disaster of cities, to find a countryside which doesn't exist any more. And the barbarians from the suburbs go back on Saturday and Sunday into town because there is nothing going on in the suburbs; you can't even get into the countryside. So that is a huge frustration. I mean it is next to sexual frustration!

One of the problems of modern towns is their structure, because instead of growing in a cellular way as all organic beings grow, when they increase they multiply instead of growing. Modern towns have increased this way, over-exceeding their mature size and thus needing artificial means of transport and communication. Virtually each town we have now is over-concentrated in the centre and over-expanded horizontally into the countryside, yet they are neither towns in the centre, nor do they preserve the countryside. Most towns have this over-dense centre and then suburbs which are literally without quality, just additions of single houses purporting to be in the countryside. Central functions are always in the centre although the houses are in the suburbs. There must be about ten million of these suburban boxes all over England, most of them one generation buildings which have absolutely no possibility of lasting longer. They will have to go or at least they will have to be replaced fairly soon. So instead of building and wrecking the little of the countryside that you still have, why not consider the suburbs as future development areas? A lot of money can be made through that. You take the normal 100 acre area occupied by a town and you find that the grid of the suburbs is often not too bad. Developing the suburbs with dense centres and with central functions will allow them to become real places and will change the town from a more centralised model to a polycentric model.

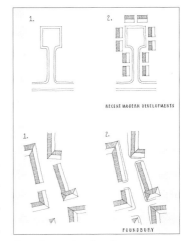

Poundbury, planning diagrams

The problem isn't only with what you build, but how you build, and the anxiety which is extremely widespread is justified. Most villages are higgledy-piggledy groups of buildings along an irregular street, usually with suburban 'arms' growing out of them, which are highly depressing. Why not round these off so that their impact is matured? There is a lot of land around existing villages in order to mature existing arms making them integral parts of the villages.

Recently I did a plan for the suburbs of Luxembourg, for the European Court, which they called the European quarter, with offices, courts, palaces and so on. It was built among motorways. I proposed to use that land for the people who work there so that they could walk to work. That plan is going to be executed by German architects. So it is interesting that you have within the built-up areas more than enough land to develop even double the size of the population.

All the talk about being forward-looking and daring about building is OK, but people want houses that

Geoffrey Broadbent

Lebbeus Woods

are traditional or at least ones that look that way. Their looks are only veneered. They are not really traditional construction. The problem is not to find new forms for these buildings, but to see how one can match what people want with what is built. Architects must give them real buildings. That is mainly a technical thing, so that the structure not only looks traditional but is a traditional form with proper walls and a proper roof, not just a display of kitsch.

Geoffrey Broadbent: The countryside is so many different kinds of things. The landscapes I find thrilling aren't the sublime ones, the big ones, the mountains and the waterfalls. The English countryside has an extremely gentle beauty in that 18th-century way and is therefore rather dull. The English countryside I like very much is where there is a great deal of human intervention in the Picturesque way. Certainly in the great landscape gardens like Stourhead and Stowe, which are the most beautiful parts of England as far as I am concerned. A great deal of the countryside owes much more to human intervention than we like to think. So what occurred to me is that Leon's view of 20th-century architecture seems to be matched by the Picturesque possibility of other kinds of 20th-century architecture. In the 18th century, you could literally take a Claude painting and translate it into a landscape. Which aspect of 20th-century art can you do that with? Not Cubism. Perhaps Abstract Expressionism. Certainly Mondrian in Holland and East Anglia. I can see lots of Mondrians everywhere.

Lebbeus Woods: I respect your dedication Leon, to your set of ideas. But I completely cannot accept this orientation towards a past which might or might not have existed. I don't even want to debate that particular point. What I am interested in is the fact that we have undergone changes qualitatively in modern life. You showed a slide of a builders' catalogue that advertised kind of pseudo-traditional houses. I find them far less horrifying intellectually and spiritually than I do the idea: 'let's be authentically traditional, let's give them authentic tradition.' I can accept a kind of hybrid, kitschy as it might be, from a builder's catalogue, as being a genuine evolution of something happening. But really to try and give them the genuine past, which won't be genuine either, is much more of a pretension – much more horrifying for me to contemplate. You say that modern architecture hasn't caught up with nuclear physics or with cybernetics and all of this revolution of thinking of the 20th century. I ask why not? Why hasn't it? Is it impossible? Is it out of the realm of possibility that the way we think about ourselves or about nature that has been developed in other fields of human thought and work can't be applied to architecture? Do we always have to go back to some imagined known order on which to base our actions?

Peter Pran: I agree with quite a lot of what Lebbeus said. I think that developments in the countryside have to be site specific in both concept and execution; they should belong to and enrich the sites. With all the alien buildings there that we hate, there has to be a new respect and a new spirit. I also think like historicists we all love the best of historical architecture. The big disagreement is, are we going to copy it or develop something new? Are we going to be known as the generation of 'copy cats'? That is what Leon wants.

There will always be people (clients, architects and critics) that want to continue to build the safe, conventional, traditional and often the banal, but it is the hope that progressive clients, architects and critics will increasingly pursue and support an innovative, creative architecture. However, in residential living – individual homes, row houses, etc – it is quite depressing to observe that in practically all countries in the world, the conventional, traditional, spiritless pitched-roof building masses of no particular architectural quality dominate 90 per cent of all one and two-storey homes for the general population; mostly it is the homes for the rich that have flat roofs or new, innovative building concepts and roof shapes. In this area, creative modern design has not yet had a substantial influence; the goal is that in the future it will. The situation is mainly the responsibility of developers, planners and architects; most of the average home owners and renters can only choose from what is offered on the market that is financially within their reach, although they can also to a degree search for the better residential designs, and take a stand. It is a false assumption to think that by repeating what has already been built in the countryside, one is honouring the past the most; the opposite is most often the truth. If we do not express new cultural statements of our own time in architecture, in the countryside (and everywhere else), it is as if we never lived. This concerns residential architecture, as well as all other buildings that are placed in the countryside, be it schools, universities, hotels, recreational centres, shopping centres, office buildings, industrial structures or museums. I think that Modern Architecture is the strongest direction in architecture today despite the historicists. Creative and courageous pursuits of, and stands for, a meaningful contemporary architecture for the countryside is our best hope of succeeding.

Peter Pran

Demetri Porphyrios: There is a group of people here who maintain that new development should focus on the densification of existing suburbs and the densification of existing dilapidated areas. A different group believes in something else. What I want to hear are their specific proposals – let's not go back to the 'pitched-vs-flat' roof discussion.

Lebbeus Woods: Yes, but I hope that the conversation we were having was not really about pitched roofs or not. It was about values. It was about a way of seeing ourselves and seeing the landscape.

Dan Cruickshank

Robert Adam: I think there is one thing that unifies what Lebbeus says and to some extent what Leon says, and this is a very critical issue for all of us. They both have visions, utterly different visions, and both to some degree believe that some aspect of control should create this vision. What emerges out of this is a real problem on the ground. One talks about development in the countryside and the relationship between vision and control; that relationship is partly a political one. If you say 'I am not going to have any more development in the countryside' and a lot of people want to live in the countryside, what actually happens is that the value of any piece of land that could possibly contain such a thing goes up and that only increases the pressure to develop. I heard the words earlier on social diversity. Well, social diversity happens through society in my opinion, not through visions. If people don't want social diversity, there is not a great deal you can do about it. I see a great division of opinion arising out of this actually very British political issue.

George Oldham: I think you are absolutely right. The important thing is to create a culture which allows that diversification and experiment to happen and visions to reach some sort of fruition. I could go on about what those forms might take. My own Arcadian visions are different to Leon's because I don't believe you need to be the ten minute walk away. I believe that you could have a string of pearls, as it were, each very different. Some with the landscape as the dominant feature within the housing, others with the housing being dominant; there could be all kinds of responses. But the important thing is we are stopping response, we are stopping creativity and that is what worries me.

Sue Clifford: There are so many different dimensions to this discussion. One is that the countryside is hugely varied and it has the capacity to take an awful lot of things and has been taking them right-face and left-face for the whole of my lifetime. The notion that the countryside is a 'nice place to live' is very quickly dispelled when you try to walk in it and you come back with spots all the way up your legs, or when you try to let your children go and play in it and find that even in a village there is nowhere for them to play. There are all of those things about the countryside that we somehow have in our heads and they simply are

Susan Clifford

James Gowan

not there in a lot of places. I grew up in a place that you would know from *Sons and Lovers* and *Women in Love*. It is a countryside that is incredibly interpenetrated by industry, very heavy industry. I should say was, because there is no longer a coal mine left and there is hardly any of Sherwood Forest left. But it is not a countryside that you are thinking of when I hear you talk. It has all these things within a ten minute walk: forest, coal mines and very dense housing. It is a countryside that, growing up there, I found incredibly rich, though not beautiful. Lawrence's own words for it were 'ugliness, ugliness, ugliness', but in the detail there was beauty.

One of the things that strikes me is that we have not talked about detail. I believe we have to have a vision and philosophy that holds true, but I also believe that we should consider detail. We have evolved as creatures that are capable of seeing a yellow leaf on a tree a long way away from us and picking out a single face in a crowd of people. Yet much of what we offer as architecture, planning and engineering is incredibly crude, crass and debilitating for our own imaginations. One of the things that people do cry out for, however, is detail, pattern and something that shows the layers.

While we turn our back on things and call them nostalgic, we forget that history is something that lives through us. History is not the past, the past is something that has gone by but history is here. Just as the genetic code is inside me and I'm part of the history of my whole family line, so we are among that sort of living history. We somehow forget that the pattern we have the capacity to create could be so rich in comparison with that which we are attempting.

I think we should work towards the notion of reinforcing diversity in its place. It is something we describe in caricature to other people when we tell them about what it is like to be here: the sort of people, languages, dialect, the sorts of things we eat and the sorts of buildings we like to live in. It is to do with local distinctiveness and so much of the abstraction we are talking about misses all of that out. We talk about a moment in time and if we can't get *zeitgeist* to talk to *genius loci* then I think we have failed.

Paul Finch: The individual perspective – could I ask James Gowan to comment?

James Gowan: In people's imaginations, the Garden of Eden is represented by the countryside and hell is represented by the city. The countryside is spiritually rather elevating. You live in your imagination but that is what sustains us so much. It certainly sustains architecture and architects, so that their imagination far outreaches their capabilities. Going back to what Leon said, the difference between Luxembourg and Britain is that Britain had an empire until very recently and also the Industrial Revolution; it has subscribed to world civilisation. The Scots with their aesthetics were popular. They did a great deal, too. Not the Luxembourgians. Think of all these red areas on the map as where Britons' imagination stretched to and the Luxembourgians' didn't. My family was modest, but my grandfathers' living room was filled with the skins and heads of wild animals and photographs of Tanganyika. In that house there were photographs of Tanganyika and that is where the garden was in their imagination. Then there was the photograph of my mother as a young girl, sitting in the house in India in the hill country, getting away from the heat. Now that is where the garden was. It extended throughout the world in their imagination. Even when they travelled to Italy that was their garden too. They were making a mess of their own country. Their own country was where they worked.

Alastair Alldridge: I live in Scotland and we have much more countryside than down here. I find that the first thing that is necessary if you talk about appropriate architecture in the countryside is to find out what sort of countryside you are talking about. What do people mean by countryside? I can count three different concepts of countryside. For the tourist it is a romantic idyll: Bonnie Prince Charlie, heather and mountains. Those who want an accessible countryside of course want fishing, shooting, motor sports and skiing. For those that live there and are the original inhabitants, the countryside is where they work; it is their croft, where they fish or grow forestry.

Now those three concepts of the countryside are, in terms of the buildings they require, almost mutually exclusive, which creates a problem for people who have to decide what is an appropriate architecture. Should the planners sit over a process of natural selection where the tourists kill off the indigenous population, or where the indigenous population see off the tourists? Or do the planners seek some sort of a consensus of architecture? The reality is that the pressure on such countryside is of course housing, and the sort of houses that people build they choose from brochures. In fact they spend the winter picking their house before they even look for the site. Now, I believe that this creates a dilemma for architects. If they are going to compete they cannot provide the number of architecturally designed houses that are required, so do they work with the people that produce these kit brochures? Is there then a generation of more responsive houses which are going to appear in brochure form? They will not be responsive to their setting, because the architect won't know where they are going to go.

Alastair Alldridge

Here I am going to side with Leon Krier. I believe that at present the population as a whole are not a part of the debate. Perhaps if people wanted to get houses that were even slightly better than the rubbish they are building at the moment, a debate could possibly begin and they would become a part of it.

Paul Finch: Leon, is log cabin syndrome the most dangerous element in Scotland?

Leon Krier: Yes, it is a fact that most speculative houses today are 25 per cent smaller than social housing standards specified in the 60s and 70s. Industry says: as long as people buy, we are going to provide – meaning provide smaller and smaller houses. This is the central problem. In England, land is owned by very few people. It is sold in huge lots, usually for large development and so a family in the country cannot buy a piece of land and build their own house. This is quite normal in Germany, France and Italy. It is changing everywhere because of industry, obviously, and Barratt have even moved to Provence.

The building market itself is the preserve of large developers who make housing, large shopping centres and so on. They are unable to make towns because towns have a certain size which cannot be exceeded and those developers will not learn to make towns; it is not their skill. And therefore I think it is very important that there are public authorities, or some public bodies, which do not represent the industry but neither are a pure and simple public authority. It could be something like they have in France which are shared private/ public capital enterprise. They design the plan of the town in the public interest and say what will happen.

In the average spec house, only about 45 per cent of what you pay, the day you get your key, is spent on the structure, probably less. So you get a kind of 45 per cent house and it is so small that you can hardly lie in bed. The houses are sold without cupboards. The show houses have a bed, but if you tried to put a cupboard into the bedroom you would be in trouble. What place is that for people to live in? It claims to be in the country, it is nowhere near the countryside. This has had several effects on the structure of public space since most of these developments are private. They usually put a gate at the entrance. They privatise the land. The cul-de-sacs are not connected. They are not an extension to the fabric of public space. This is privatisation, not only of housing but also of shopping. There are two shops; they are also privately owned and they close the door at six o'clock, so the only centrality you have is for shopping. The erosion of public space in those new developments is absolutely tragic.

All of the people who move to these new spaces have to use old towns because they have no centrality. Centrality and urbanity only survive in old towns, so instead of overlooking those old towns we must create new towns which are real places and which have public spaces as good as the old ones do. How to do this

is a project. It is just not good enough to say we should explore different possibilities and *zeitgeist* and so on, you have to have a solution. Society asks you: 'How are you going to build a house? How wide are the streets? Are they parallel or are they concave? What is the texture?' These are technical, practical problems. There is a market out there for people who transform the landscape. We have to tell them: 'this is the size of the development, this is the nature of it and those are the materials'. There are already regulations. Why not use regulations which make places instead of just suburban garbage?

George Oldham: The last contributions have really stirred something up in me. It is actually worse than Leon says it is. Not the 45 per cent house, it is generally the 33 per cent house for a speculative developer and you have got to ask yourself why that is. There are two major reasons. The first is the politics of deprivation, of being unable to get at the countryside to build, which creates artificial land values and forms a running sore which is a disgrace. The other is the way we build in this country.

Christopher Martin

We build generally for between £35 and £40 a square foot, using developers' terms, using bricks and mortar and cavities and all that. Whereas over in the States, for example, they build nice timber-framed houses which they retail, triple-glazed and the like, at something like £25 per square foot. I'm not surprised that people in Scotland sit around in their crofts of a winter evening and look at these pretty pictures of kit houses because they actually represent incredible value for money, compared to the developers' houses and the houses that we try to build in our cities. The question that we must ask ourselves as architects is: How on earth can we translate the mundane that is in those pages into something which is really worthwhile for people? We should do this, rather than spend time worrying about whether we are putting an 18th-century or a 1930s skin on it.

Dirk Kohler

Christopher Martin: The thing that stuns me is that nothing has happened in planning terms since the 50s, but anyone who has kept an eye on the countryside will know that immeasurable change has happened in the countryside over the last 40 years. It is largely irreversible. The other fact that was mentioned was that one per cent of the countryside would absorb all our building needs. That sounds reassuringly like a helpful statistic, but not only are those buildings irreversible, their position in the countryside makes them very, very sensitive. A building put in the wrong place at the wrong time can practically damage a county. So if you are suggesting that somehow they can be scattered across the countryside and a thousand flowers can grow and present a challenge for *zeitgeist* or whatever, then I am utterly opposed to you.

It does not seem to me that the *Essex Design Guide* has been quite the environmental disaster that it has been claimed to be. And the reason why local planning authorities are so nervous about giving the sort of edge to architecture that Max Hutchinson would favour is because of experience, and the consequences of diverging from those guidelines. Having said that, I would certainly agree that there is something terribly etiolating about country living, about thatch, about good taste, about those sort of curtains, about those sort of gardens and about the sort of pictures that hang on those sort of walls. It is very enervating if a culture depends too much on having that kind of fabric around it. I contradict myself a bit. Somehow I believe one has got to be able to express, with imagination, the traditional needs of what people want in the countryside. I don't know what the answer to that is, but I think it is something to do with people like us who largely do live in towns entering into this debate. This issue is absolutely vital to Londoners who haven't seen the countryside, in the same way that what happens to the blue whale is important to people who have no experience of whaling.

Paul Finch: Max Hutchinson, I think I gathered that you were in favour of a one per cent club for putting houses into the countryside. Could you comment on whether we are simply looking at a failure of

OPPOSITE ABOVE AND BELOW:
Willy Harbinson of the Percy Thomas Partnership, Housing at Luccombe; Stephen Mattick, 16th-century barn converted into two dwellings, Ickleton, Cambs

Mary Creswell

David Taylor

imagination in terms of planning in the countryside, both from a political and a cultural point of view. Are we simply frightened by the idea that we should identify the land, compulsory purchase it at agricultural values and then sell it to individual people who can build houses in the context of a public masterplan?

Maxwell Hutchinson: Well, firstly, I am shocked by the idea that we are given the *Daily Mail Book of House Plans* as a model and then told that this is what people want. It's all that is offered to people. When developers do attempt to build some more interesting houses, like those designed by the late Eric Lyons or Jeremy Dickson, they are absolutely lapped up. I would like to know from George Oldham why, when he went to a volume house builder, we didn't suddenly see his benign cultured influence on the output of that builder? If the industry was made by architects to be more aware of the alternatives which can be provided by architects, then I believe that they would be lapped up by the house buying public. That, I think, is demonstrated for example at the Milton Keynes Energy Park where there is a variety of very progressive houses, all of which were snapped up the minute they were made available.

Maybe one reason we don't have more quality is that the individual plot of land is almost unavailable in this country. Where individual plots of land, either in the town or the country, are available we see advances in house design. Most individuals who have the privilege of a bespoke house normally opt for something which is individual and progressive, expressing their own belief and seldom or never represented by the kind of imagery we see on the cover of the *Daily Mail House Plans*. So we do need planning policies which make the individual plot of land more readily available. I believe that if they were, we could see a developing culture of the individual house which would change our national expectation.

Leon Krier: The interesting thing is I am not proposing the *Daily Mail* catalogue as a model; it merely illustrates what people want. They don't want Mies van der Rohe houses.

Maxwell Hutchinson: You did say, did you not, that that is what people want and it is only a shame that they aren't built by traditional means.

Leon Krier: Yes, but if they buy a car they don't buy a thatched car.

Maxwell Hutchinson: No, but they buy a car which I think is stylistically rather out of date.

Paul Finch: Since you have mentioned the motor car I would like to ask David Taylor of Alan Baxter Engineers to speak on this very important subject, and to discuss what he calls 'the dominance of the car'.

David Taylor: The story of the countryside in the 20th century is inextricably linked to the development and use of the motor car. From its beginnings as a rich man's toy the influence of the car has grown to the point where it now dominates all our lives. At Alan Baxter & Associates we have given a great deal of thought to how we can civilise the car, essentially by changing the relationship between roads and the built fabric of our towns and villages.

The story starts with the development of the motor car in the 1880s. From that time we can trace the growing influence of the car, to a stage in the 1920s when it became a major influence on planning policy in this country. The 20s saw the start of zoning for commercial, industrial and residential uses and the emergence of the influence of the traffic engineer on the way we actually plan our built environment. That influence rapidly grew through to the 1950s, when the first motorways were constructed in this country, and thus to the era of major comprehensive redevelopments in the 1960s. It is present much more subtly today in smaller-scale developments such as recent suburban housing schemes.

During this period one key thing has happened. The roles of the architect, the urban planner and the traffic engineer have slowly drifted apart with each taking his own course. Traffic engineering has gradually taken the dominant role.

The basic approach to traffic engineering that has been developed over the past few years is hierarchical. At the top is the motorway system, such as the M25, a clear motorway rolling through the countryside, often doubling up as a car park on Monday mornings. Then there are our A-roads where the same broad design logic is applied, and lower down the scale are our country roads and our suburban estates. But within this hierarchical approach the basic engineering logic which is applied to motorways is also applied to small streets and country lanes. All our modern housing is really designed around the car – the movement of the car, sight lines for the car and the general segregation of the car from the built environment. This is wrong. We need to put our built environment and our countryside first, and then place the roads or the medium that the traffic will use between the built spaces, so that they are actually much less dominant. In current developments housing layouts designed around traffic-engineered cul-de-sacs impose a totally alien pattern on our built development, completely different to the way in which our towns and settlements have developed historically.

Barren car parking devoid of life

Urban square, Cognac

At Poundbury, where we are working with Leon Krier, we devised a much softer approach for traffic engineering; one that uses the space between the buildings, so that the car plays a much less dominant role than in other developments. This shows how the whole process of designing for the car can be rethought.

First of all, on the contentious subject of parking, if you take up to about 12 cars parked together they can look all right so long as the environment they are in is dominant over them. Cars parked in a car park with trees and buildings around them often blend into the background, but every so often we see situations where a car park has been created to serve a local sports area. Here space has been provided for 50 cars, but no attention has been paid to landscaping. On a Sunday afternoon it's full, it's quite a lively place, but during the rest of the week it's completely dead space, devoid of interest. This can be contrasted to a similar area in Cognac in France, a marvellous, beautiful town. Here we have a car park that truly can be called a car park, 50 or so cars situated amongst trees in a tightly built environment. The car is actually blending into the background so it's not seen as being the dominant feature. Of course, being France, this area also doubles for many other events, and when cars aren't there it is actually an extremely pleasant place to sit. So multi-use parking spaces must be a good thing. Too often we see in our housing developments areas of barren courtyard where the space is solely designed for the car. I believe that we can use these places much more creatively and in some instances mix the types of use completely.

Another example of how seriously we take car parking in this country is that our urban roads are lined with yellow lines, making them completely clear of parked cars. I'm not saying that this is a bad idea, particularly if you live on a busy road, but of course this actually detracts from the road very often. Compare this to an example in Britanny, where the road wasn't quite wide enough to allow parking at the side, so the French allowed parking half on the pavement, half on the road. A very relaxed approach, much more so than is seen in this country.

The second question is just how the speed of the car is controlled in our developments. Obviously on motorways and large roads speed is important – on them we want to get somewhere as safely and quickly as possible. But when we come to housing developments or local rural roads, speed is not a major consideration, and what is needed is a place where pedestrians are dominant. Typical recent developments control the speed of cars by the use of cul-de-sacs or a hierarchy of roads to inhibit the actual flow of the vehicles. This generates an engineered pattern of development. At Poundbury we have dealt with this problem in a slightly different way. Our approach is to devise the street pattern that is required by looking

Clare Melhuish

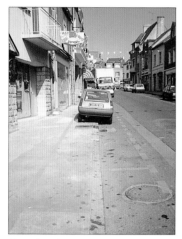

Casual parking in Brittany

at the buildings first, and then to use this to generate events or places along the street to interrupt the flow of the traffic, effectively to calm it. By placing events at regular intervals you can keep traffic speeds down to acceptable levels, typically 20mph or less. So speed can be controlled within new built environments without the need for adding traffic calming to conventional highway engineering.

Finally, a word about materials: since in all of our built spaces very subtle changes in the use of materials can affect the whole way that an area is perceived. All too often we see areas of barren tarmac, with hard concrete kerbs defining the edges of roads. Some of our villages have changed considerably over the past 40 years. Just after the War grass verges actually came down and touched the road, but these have been replaced by kerbs in many places. For me this subtle change has taken the road from being a place which was just space between buildings to actually defining a place where the car has its dominance. Do we really need that kerb? The use of tarmac with some stone, subtly blended creates a very pleasing effect at relatively minimal cost. People walking through this space feel at ease. In Brittany there are many examples of the use of stone, with stone kerbs and asphalt; very simple techniques, but creating very pleasant spaces carefully detailed so as to avoid the effect of a cold barren road.

The relationship between cars and buildings is now as much a problem in villages and small towns as it is in our major cities. The techniques described here represent a reassertion of the importance of buildings and places, and the use of buildings as a way of controlling the car. Without such measures, conventional traffic engineering will continue to be a scourge to the countryside.

Paul Finch: Thank you very much. Moving on from the specific impact of the car, I am going to ask David Fleming, who is an environmental consultant, to comment on the environmental issues in this debate.

David Fleming: We have to put the whole of this debate about planning and land-use into the context of environmental change. We tend to suppose that the future will continue to be fairly much like the present, in most essentials. But we are almost certainly wrong about this, since 'change' is itself changing: the future will not consist of more of the same – more wealth, more people, more cars, more opportunities for the architectural profession. It will bring breaks in the trends, shocks which computers, with their tendency to project current trends, are likely to miss. That is to say, we are entering the Age of Discontinuity.

There are several factors which must be considered. Firstly, we should not be planning for a society in which people use cars as their primary means of transport, because carbon taxes will be introduced in the next decade which will make driving progressively more expensive. People will then want their places of work, school and shops, their friends, relatives and even holidays to be within easy walking distance rather than feasible driving distance. Secondly, as Clive mentioned earlier, the present food surplus could change into a food deficit as the climate changes, bringing heat, drought and ultra-violet radiation, reduced resistance to disease and predators, and poor harvests. If this should happen, one response could be a renewed emphasis on 'extensification' – low-input agriculture, which is hungry for land, and which would provide an urgent alternative use for the land now being set aside into golf courses, parks and paint-war-game ranges. Finally, we can already see many signs of the most enormous social stress in the towns. Unemployment, crime and vandalism continue to rise, and we have so far made no progress towards solving these problems. When we do, we will find ourselves in unfamiliar territory.

This may seem an unduly pessimistic and alarmist approach. But the fact that these things *may* happen means that we cannot be lumbered with a planning policy which assumes that they *won't*. Instead we should base planning and land-use policy on three principles, those of integration, economy and quality.

Integration means designing (or adapting) communities so that members can satisfy the highest possible proportion of their needs without leaving the area. The principle that a particular function should have a particular (separate) location has been extremely destructive; it has led to a fragmentation of our lives between work, shopping, recreation and home; it has meant that places, and even our relationships, have become defined by function rather than valued in themselves. So, instead of thinking about the houses we build (in which people all too often live in communal loneliness) we should be thinking about the communities which we help to come into being. As regards economy, the society for which we are now building will have to use solar power to the maximum, keep the consumption of fossil fuel to the minimum, reduce waste, reuse packaging and materials wherever possible, and recycle materials. This adds up to an architectural and planning agenda in its own right: energy-efficient buildings, short transport distances, recycling facilities, the treatment and use of organic waste, and measures which save on the vast resource cost of vandalism and crime prevention by some form of community participation in keeping its own peace. It means local 'economy' in the fullest sense – better results for less input. Finally, the idea of quality in architecture and planning has been coming back powerfully for two decades, after a post-war period when the emphasis was more on quantity, productivity and systems building techniques than on quality. But there is still a long way to go.

David Fleming

These three principles – integration, economy and quality – mean in practice that it makes no sense to think about architecture and planning in terms of 'giving consumers what they want'. Consumers tend to misinterpret the choices confronting them; ideas of what makes a reasonable driving-distance to work are based on pre-carbon-tax petrol prices. Ideas of the desirable home give too great an emphasis to the quality of the home and too little to the quality of the community in which it is set. Taken to the limit, consumer sovereignty in housing means unending suburbia and huge environmental damage, offering neither the benefit of privacy nor that of community. At the limit, consumer sovereignty turns into consumer defeat.

Pierre D'Avoine

Paul Finch: Sir, can I ask you a question? Do you imagine that this will have implications for building form: I mean do you think buildings are going to look very different in 20 years time?

David Fleming: They will have to, because there are EC regulations coming up for building design – for energy conservation – so in many ways they are going to be different. Clients will want that. As energy costs rise, it will be very much cheaper to design an energy-efficient home rather than a traditional home.

Paul Finch: I would like to bring in Ian Ritchie about transport and the notion of town versus country and the differences about that.

Ian Ritchie: It is very difficult because one's mind actually races a bit with the diversity and complexity of the actual issues that are at stake. At this Forum it also seems a prerequisite that one should say where one grew up. From the age of nought, I grew up in Stenning, which was then a village of about 4,000 people and is now some 12,000, I understand. My mobility was foot. Dr Beeching axed the railway, but we caught it just in time to get to Brighton, at the age of seven. I think the most important thing whilst I was in Brighton was not the Nash terraces or the squares in Hove; it was in fact the sea. This leaves me with the thought that we've talked about the countryside and we've talked about the town, but we haven't talked about the coast. The third stage was 30 plus, having come from Brighton by car to London, where I don't own a car any longer; things are more accessible if one is here because of diversity.

Where does that leave me today in the debate? Recently Demetri Porphyrios and I were invited to Magdalen College to do an exercise in the College deer park. Now, was that country or town? My approach was about hierarchy of scale and fractural geometry in the context of the ambivalence of Magdalen College, which picks up on a point mentioned earlier. It is whether you are on private or public land in England. At

25

Ian Ritchie

Victor Arwas

Magdalen College, my first sensation was that I never knew if I was inside or outside the College for much of the time, although I had gone inside the walls. There was an ambiguity about the cloisters; doors didn't appear until many strides later and up staircases. The Fellows interpreted Demetri's scheme as Tradition and mine as Modernity. The Fellows ranged from 25 year olds to geriatrics; and I understand from the bursar that the majority of the geriatrics went for the Modernity, while the 30-year-old younger fellows voted for Demetri, which is quite interesting.

Magdalen College parallels another area of the housing debate which is the business park. The growth of the business park I find an anathema in today's society, because it is a simple reflection of the motor car and of private mobility. Do we accept the car as inevitable? I tend to sympathise with those who believe that in the not too distant future the city will not be a place for the car.

Paul Finch: Thank you very much. George?

George Oldham: I think people have the idea that I am saying 'let rip'; perhaps I am even going to further that view of the Oldham thesis. I remember the '72 Commoner/Peccei debate at the RIBA conference about limits to growth, and I don't really buy the Malthusian theory. I don't think we are heading for a catastrophe. We always find ways of getting through things. I don't condemn personal mobility and the motor car. I think it has been absolutely fantastic. We just need to look at it and approach it rationally.

We must differentiate between what is the urban experience and what Arcadia is like. It is perhaps a more rural experience. I am not frightened of motorways: Glasgow to Manchester used to take ten hours, now it takes about four, and it is a much more pleasant experience with Beethoven on the radio. It actually opens up some fabulous countryside to me which I didn't see before. It expands my life rather than diminishing it. What we need to do is get practical solutions which don't pander to the bureaucrats.

Paul Finch: Can I bring in Susan Denyer at this point, for a National Trust perspective?

Susan Denyer: Can I comment, first of all, as someone who lives and works in the countryside, and in a countryside in the north of England which is not prosperous, and is of marginal importance agriculturally? For houses to work in the countryside, they have got to work on three levels. In a sense they have got to look right. They have got to satisfy two other criteria: who is going to live in them and what they are going to do? They have got to work aesthetically, socially and economically. They have got to be for people who should be there, can be there and have a living to make in the countryside. Ideally they have got to be part of a viable countryside. The countryside has always changed in the past but it is faced with much more far reaching and irreversible changes than before.

The lives of the people who live in the countryside are no longer controlled from within the region where they live, or indeed from this country. There are forces impinging on farmers and everyone who works and lives in the countryside from much further afield. Perhaps even more so are the consequences of the present GATT negotiations. So I think that we have to look at a countryside which is not evolving regionally or internationally, but is part of a much bigger global problem. We can't allow it to develop in the way it developed in the past from within, and organically. There have to be controls to achieve what we want to achieve out of the countryside. At the moment we have positive and negative controls. The negative controls say 'you must not build here'. The positive controls are endeavouring to keep farmers in the countryside by propping up the economy and the farms on which they work. We must have both sides if we want to create or keep the mixed communities that created our countryside in the first place.

Many communities are dying on their feet – farmers aren't making a living. They are becoming communities which are only farmers, commuters and retired people. They are not the mixed communities that were the essence of English countryside in the past. In the future farmers will find it difficult to make the whole of their livelihood from their farming. We will have to look at measures to enable farmers to have other sources of income; workshops perhaps, or such things as 'tele-cottages' which are much in debate at the moment.

There have always been constraints in the past. If you look in depth at most villages it wasn't a 'free for all'. Rules dictated how houses should be built: whether they should rise from an old/new site and which way they should face. The challenge is how to adjust the positive and negative rules to allow the sort of development that we want. Somebody earlier on mentioned trying to control this through materials and I think this is going to have to happen. But I don't think it should just be negative; there should be some positive intervention as well. Architects and planners should suggest how this should be achieved. Farm buildings are a more dominant part of the countryside than houses and there is a need to develop not just satisfactory houses but satisfactory farm buildings which are needed now to accommodate all sorts of processes that weren't even thought of in the past. How would you design a slurry tank, and so on? These are all urgent problems that need to be solved, but we haven't got three generations to solve them.

I don't think just specifying materials and site and hoping that some marvellous solution will be reached will work. There will have to be intervention, and positive, to suggest how these challenges can be met.

Susan Denyer

Acorn Restoration, Perton Farm Telehamlet, Herefordshire

Maxwell Hutchinson: Our attention has been drawn to the Department of Transport, if only it were that. It is in fact the Department of Roads which has a self-interest and therefore promotes the use of roads, which is why we don't have an integrated transport policy in England. It is no wonder that the motorways were built and that we have roads in rural areas because there is no way in which our railway, air and road transport systems are integrated into one holistic view about the way in which we move. Meanwhile the old tilting advanced passenger train rots in a siding at Crewe station. A first class train fare from London to Manchester is £125, a first class railway fare from Rome to Venice is only £52. We have started to face up to those issues in the city. Both Ian Ritchie and I can prove that you can live very satisfactorily in London without a motor car. I have tried it in the country, it is absolutely impossible. We see how the Metro train service has completely changed the way in which the city of Newcastle has been used. I am sure we will see the light tram system change the way Manchester is used. I don't think we should give up the idea of integrating new transport mechanisms into the countryside as well; accepting the inevitability of the car is very dangerous in itself. If we look at other means of moving people about then we stand some chance of moderating the fearful inevitability of the dominance of the car.

Lebbeus Woods: Two of the presentations this afternoon – by Susan Denyer and David Fleming – have been in a way the most telling of the future as it is shaping up. Their vision is that we are heading towards big central planning, big distant global control of the environment. The spectre of this global control is raised here. Maybe there are 'good reasons' for it. I am terrified by this prospect, because even though the reasons offered are humanistic and good, the reality is that politicians are not operating on that basis. They are operating on contingencies which have to do with multinational corporations, with all kind of dirty business and politics – big money and big global money.

What worries me, Leon, is that your feelings for a kind of unity seem to comply with that control picture. It seems to me that I can take David Fleming and Susan Denyer's views, and your idea of a kind of total planning architecture, and put them together into something fairly totalitarian – not in the old style, but in the soft new slick style of packaging and marketing which is nonetheless tyrannical. If your ideas about planning aren't tinged with that kind of autocratic totalitarian dimension, I would like to hear about it.

Julian Bicknell

Ketterwell, Yorkshire

Julian Bicknell: The thing that concerns and interests me most is that there was one item in your agenda which seemed to be missing, because you spoke of the aesthetic, social and economic. The thing that was missing was the geographical. There is a question about where you put buildings, because I think it is unquestionably the case that there will have to be buildings put somewhere. Now lay that against the idea of Arcadia which Leon Krier was talking about and Demetri mentioned before. The mythic ideal which so many of us would like to imagine is something to do with enjoying the countryside as city folk. This goes back to a splendid issue of *AD* called the 'Edge of the Forest' in which there were a series of essays suggesting that the ideal place for man to live is on the edge of the forest, sharing both in the mystery of that dark and unknown world and the clarity and openness of what we now think of as countryside. The essence of this was that the ideal is on the edge. Krier touched on this, claiming that the magic places for all these things to happen are going to be the edges between what we might like to call countryside at the moment and what we might like to call town or suburbia, or whatever it might be. Those edges have the unique characteristic that biological systems always exploit, which is that they find an area where the difference already exists and explore those differences. They do this in a way which responds to the complexity, the depth, the subtlety and the volume of all those edge conditions.

The intriguing thing is that at the end of the 20th century we are beginning to have a series of disciplines under a general heading of practical geometry, which allow us to look at very small, very individual cases in terms of general rules. So it seems to be that there is a possibility, at least intellectually if not in real life, to make the bridge between the particularities of rules and the generalities of political control from the EC or whatever it might be. So that the only summary I can make is that we should look for places where the knife can be put in and try to find out with greater accuracy than has ever been possible before, how you exercise your surgical skills.

Robert Adam: There was an apocalyptic vision of the motor car and loss of energy in the 70s. It didn't actually happen. That is the worry about visions. I don't think the thing is to ban the car, prevent the means of transport, because it would be a very difficult thing to take away; when you've let the genie out of the bottle, you've given people a taste of something.

Paul Finch: Christopher Day, does organic growth imply slow growth? Or what happens to the idea of organic growth if you suddenly start to speed it all up, under the pressure of external events?

Christopher Day: If it is to remain organic it must be related to an appropriate rate of change, it must be related to time factors. What I really want to say is: am I correct in thinking that this Forum is about development in the countryside? Because if that is so, it seems to me that there are far more important questions to talk about than stylistic or personal oppositions of stand point, or questions of whether it is better to live in the town or the countryside. The fact is that if we don't have a countryside, lives in towns are unsustainable. If we didn't have towns our countryside as we know it would be so radically changed that it would be unrecognisable. So the issue is, how can we bring the two relationships together and how can development be beneficial? At the present moment, in this country in particular, we have a settlement model whereby towns are supported by life flow from the countryside. We don't really know where our food is coming from and we don't know where our waste products are going to. This is the basic attitude from which all our ecological abuse stems.

How can we think of the relation between human activities and the natural world as an asset and a heritage, in the way that we can look at old settlement patterns that we can't recreate in the spirit with which they were built? We have to find new ways. There are new ways, I am absolutely convinced of it. I have

KILBEES FARM

John Melvin

Stuart Page

also been working in this direction myself and this is surely the substance at the heart of this debate.

Stuart Page: So far the majority of the discussion has gone on about style and the imposition of urban values on the countryside, without understanding how the countryside really is supporting us all. It is as vital to our welfare as the city. Technology gives the lie to some of the rural myths that have been discussed. Today a computer-controlled tractor delivers computer-controlled amounts of fertiliser to the computer-controlled soil and the mechanically-controlled level of plough. All this is far more advanced than many of the vehicles that we drive around in. I have felt alienated by the discussion of style and architectural value on what is basically central to all our existence. I think if we are considering ways that the land or the countryside has developed, we have to forget Arcadia. It isn't Arcadia.

John Melvin: I think it is important that we don't set up false dichotomies between the town and the countryside, because the forces are so huge and multinational, forcing industry out of the city. The city is no longer going to be the great manufacturing centre. Most people want desperately to get out of the city, the pull of Arcadia is very much a city problem. How do you cope with being in the city and the consequences of people wanting to get out?

Like Utopia, Arcadia is an ideal. While Utopia is rationalist and urban, Arcadia is its antithesis – the countryside idealised to which urban man seeks escape from values that are merely rational. Arcadia is the 20th century's outpost of the city linked invisibly to the metropolis by technology and visibly by tarmac.

From the time of the Enclosures in the 18th century, the countryside has been man-made. It will continue to be so, no longer serving agriculture but the rapacious demands of the leisure industry and the *arriviste* dictates of the weekend huntsmen. If Arcadia is the true expression of today's city, any consideration of its architecture will have to embrace the former urban heart as Arcadia is the reverse of the same urbanised coin. As we green the city and bring metropolitan values to the countryside, both the country and the city become gradations of one sensibility. In the city the residual historic core will carry an increased burden of our history and memory which will require considerable care to retain. It may well be that Arcadian man will repair to the town to find his weekend retreat. The aesthetic of Arcadia will draw upon our national propensity for the picturesque, the historical, the literary and the eclectic. Thus we should perhaps develop into a conscious art-form the multi-viewpoint perspective with its telescoping of sequential time and space.

Historic precursors to this sensibility are Nash at Blaise Hamlet, Baillie Scott at Hampstead Garden Suburb and Hampstead Garden Suburb itself, which can arguably lay claim to be the finest architectural environment we have created. Also, if you go round America some of the best 20th-century environments are the suburbs. What we have got to do is learn how to find out what it is that people are looking for and make their architectural environments better.

Leon Krier: Let me ask why people want suburbs if they don't like trees. The middle class rich suburbs in the US have fantastic trees, whereas the English seem to hate trees. Suburban gardens are absolutely dreadful and to call that a nature preserve is hilarious! They cut anything which grows taller than this table. It is ridiculous. I think people actually hate suburbs because they are neither country nor town.

Michael Morris: I am sure I could find suburbs for you that show very important tree growth.

Clive Aslet: This is a good time to summarise, I think, because some of the discussion has been suffering from the discontinuity David Fleming mentioned. To go back to the very beginning, when I said that I was against development in the countryside, I didn't intend to imply that I have a nostalgic view of the countryside or that I was against change. Many of the changes that have happened are actually for the better: for example, planting new hedges and woodland. The problem is that many of the changes we have been discussing aren't reversible. One change we haven't dwelt on much is that surveys now suggest that two thirds of people in Britain want to spend their recreation time in the countryside. At the beginning of the century people would have said the seaside, because that is where trains took them and the seaside towns were developed to entertain large numbers. Now people can drive out in their cars and take their recreation in the countryside.

In the first half of the symposium we talked mainly about houses and one has to recognise that one person's nice place to live might be somebody else's eyesore. This is touched on in the question of tourism and houses in the highlands. I am sure it's right that we need more footpaths but I wouldn't agree with Leon that people can't get into the countryside. Over the last few days I have been to Colchester for lunch and driven back to London for dinner. So there is an enormous mobility round the countryside, which rather underlies the point that perhaps the differences that we perceive between the town and country aren't always as great as we make out. I don't agree that there is evidence for Max Hutchinson's suggestion that villages need to expand to survive because more houses in a village don't necessarily secure more services. Very often people who come to live there operate their cars like everyone else does.

Clive Aslet

Maxwell Hutchinson: I didn't just say houses. I did actually say education and industry. We need to expand in general.

Clive Aslet: I would like to share with you the results of a recent survey. *Country Life* wrote to every MP asking various questions about the countryside and the arts. One of the questions was: What do you think the best use of the land which is currently surplus to agricultural requirements should be? They were given the choice of four options. One was tree planting. One was increased leisure use. One was open space. One was new houses. We had 170 responses to the survey. They mostly tended to be Conservative. The Labour Party had decided not to fill out any surveys before the election in case anyone found out what they thought. The results were 80 per cent in favour of tree planting, while open space was 35 to 41 per cent. Even amongst this largely Conservative group of MPs only 20 per cent voted for house building. That is going to be a problem for those people who believe that two million more houses are needed.

The viewing of the Alexander Calder Exhibition after the International Forum

Also, we didn't fully address the geographical problem that Julian Bicknell mentioned. Because the fact of the matter is that none of our new villages have got planning permission.

We have talked about the myth of Arcadia and I would agree that it certainly is a myth, one of the few shared myths we have left in this country. What surprises me is that it is a myth of relatively recent growth. I was reading Osbert Lancaster's memoirs recently. I had imagined that having grown up at the turn of the century he would almost certainly have come from a country house background or have gone to the country at weekends. But he was brought up in Notting Hill and his family never went into the country for the weekends because they always went to church, a forgotten tradition of upper middle-class life. That caused me great surprise as I had always assumed that the weekend had been a central part of British life since the beginning of the century. The myth has been fuelled by many different things, one of which is the existence of *Country Life*, but the other is the so-called shelter magazines writing about the country. Of course I plead guilty. Architecturally the most studied building type in this country is the country house. Prisons and town halls haven't had nearly as much attention. If there were more studies like Mark Girouard's book on English towns, showing that in previous centuries there was far more vital life in the towns in this country as opposed to the countryside than one would ever have imagined, I think that myth might be mitigated.

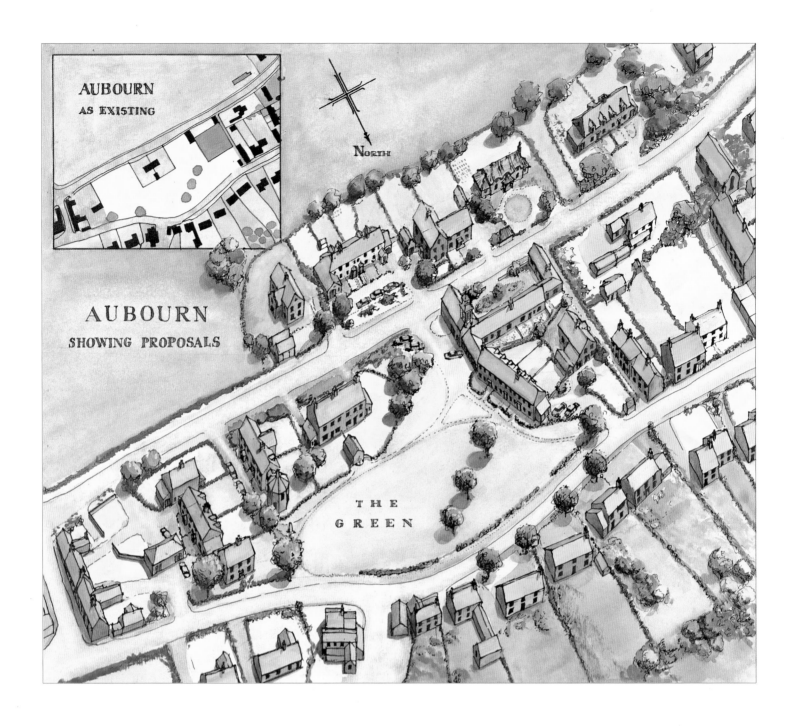

AUBOURN
AS EXISTING

NORTH

AUBOURN
SHOWING PROPOSALS

THE
GREEN

Murray John, bird's-eye view and elevation, village of Aubourn, Lincolnshire. Much thought has gone into views from houses – each house should have two views from its windows – and the relation of private gardens to open space. The circulation of pedestrians and the routing of new paths have also been carefully thought out to enhance feelings of community and security

GILES WORSLEY
RURAL HOUSING DESIGN
The Search for the Middle Way

Thanks to the planning system, the idealised image of the English countryside portrayed by photographs from 1952, the year of the Queen's accession to the throne has, to a surprising extent, survived, to be celebrated in a thousand picture books and tourist posters. Except for the odd lost tree, the odd white line, the photographs could be recreated exactly. For, in broad terms, planning has largely been effective in controlling unnecessary development in the countryside. EM Forster's *Howard's End,* published in 1910, painted a bleak picture of the spreading tentacles of urbanisation; and to see what England could have been like one only has to go to a country like Italy with much weaker planning controls. Happily the planning laws of the 1930s and 40s cauterised those tentacles. Driving through a county like Buckinghamshire one can still see the high tide of this development; strange ribbons of housing and out of place factories marooned in the countryside when the planning system suddenly changed like driftwood left by the tide. But in many ways this idealised image has only been able to survive as the result of an almost Faustian pact between planners and developers. The green belts, the picturesque villages and much open countryside – as long as it is not too close to towns which do not have green belts – have generally been left untouched, thanks to the protection given to them by the Town and Country Planning Act of 1947, but the rest has been effectively sacrificed. This is particularly true of villages, which are rapidly being divided into two types. On the one hand are the *pretty* villages fit for television commercials, only affordable by the middle classes, often overrun by tourists and doomed to be preserved in aspic with all the social and economic consequences that entails. On the other are *working* villages, swamped by new housing, where there may be some controls over how much is built but apparently few over its quality or impact.

To seek the cause of this divide one needs to go back a long way, probably to the Picturesque tradition. To an astonishing extent this late 18th-century concept still dominates our aesthetic judgement and hence what we deem worthy of protection. Thus the picturesque stone villages of the Dales and Howardian Hills of Yorkshire are carefully protected (one only

has to watch 'All Creatures Great and Small' on television to see what I mean), but the brick villages in the *boring* Vale of York (which are often equally attractive) have in many cases been effectively abandoned to the developer.

Villages must, however, be allowed to grow and change and there is no reason why it should be accepted that that change should necessarily be for the worse visually. Villages have never been static. Sometimes they have grown. Sometimes they have shrunk. Sometimes they have disappeared altogether, although rural depopulation and the shrinking village are not really a problem in this country, unlike in many rural areas of the Continent. Sadly, however, the attitude of the classic *nimby* is quite understandable. Most new developments in villages have been at the expense of their attractiveness. People who buy houses in pretty villages, particularly retired people, professionals working some distance away or weekenders, with no personal incentive to accept change are therefore almost inevitably driven to oppose it. But there are architects and developers who can build in a way that certainly does not detract from a village and may actually improve it. There are even private individuals and developers who are prepared to encourage them. Unfortunately they are exceptional and their work is largely unsung. If their example were emulated then we could chart a middle way for the English village based on sensitive beneficial development, not on blanket bans or abject surrender to development.

The key lies, inevitably, with the planning system: developers, private individuals, architects and builders work within the parameters this sets. It is the planning system which decides what is permitted. To a large extent it determines what is or is not economic. Sadly, many of the essential planning principles which make the work of these architects so effective in a village context run contrary to planning guidelines and assumptions. One can find numerous sensible schemes which have been stopped by such guidelines. But there are planners who are not satisfied with current orthodoxies and are prepared to encourage innovative thought. I just wish there were more.

Two factors can be seen as determining the

Malcolm Tempest, Roseberry Green in the village of North Stainley, North Yorkshire

Stephen Mattick, new houses at Store by Clare, Suffolk

Stephen Mattick, re-built cattle shed, Hinxton, Cambs

success or failure of new village housing. The first is planning – the relationship between individual houses and groups of houses and between the open spaces and roads which surround and service them. The second is architecture – that is the appearance of individual homes, their proportions, fenestration, materials, sensitivity to the local vernacular. At the moment most new village housing fails on both counts.

The sad truth about most housing is that its planning seems to owe little to the villages in which it is being imposed. Small wonder that it seems so alien or that its impact is so corrosive. Rather than identifying the strengths of traditional village planning and then adapting those in the light of modern needs, a completely different set of principles – suburban principles – based essentially on a reaction to urban problems, are imposed.

The heroic age of the town planner was at the end of the last century and the beginning of this one, as the profession struggled with the problems of over-crowding, poverty and disease in city slums. Quite rightly it fought for lower densities, gardens and light. The product of these struggles was the triumph of the suburb – made of low density, generally detached or semi-detached housing set well apart from places of work – as the almost universal pattern for new housing. This is certainly true of the countryside where new housing developments, whether they are massive new settlements or relatively small additions, are essentially suburban in plan. But is there not something strange about the fact that the way we design in the countryside at the end of the 20th century derives from planning assumptions generated by the conditions of our cities a century ago? After all, we are no longer struggling to fight cholera and tuberculosis and it is a very exceptional house today which does not have running water and drainage.

There is, of course, another reason why suburban-type developments have become standard. Onto the basic assumption in favour of suburban densities has been grafted the pre-eminence of the motor car. When it comes to planning new housing develop-ments the layout is almost entirely determined by the regulations of the Highways Engineer. It is these that determine the width of roads and the pavements, dictate their endless serpentine bends, insist on all those roundabouts, demand that houses are set back from the road to allow off street parking, turning spaces and double garages, not to mention concrete curbs and different coloured road surfaces to mark private space. The idea that the motor car is only one element in a complex pattern of planning seems to have been forgotten. And, of course, for the lazy developer and planner the very standardisation of

planning demanded by the rules of the Highways Engineer has much in its favour. It means that the same layout and pattern of housing can be repeated endlessly regardless of situation with substantial resulting economies of scales.

Of course the Highways Engineer has a point; one certainly wants to minimise traffic congestion and the possibility of accidents, but at what cost? Safety has become such a sacred cow that its demands are seldom questioned, but are we not suffering from overkill? Is it really essential to have roads wide enough for two dustcarts to pass at 20mph? At the moment there is no effective way to challenge the Highways Engineer and our villages have suffered accordingly and will continue to suffer until the substantial costs inherent in his demands are made clear. What is needed is some form of environmental audit. This is a fashionable concept at the moment, usually raised when major schemes are being considered, one thinks of Twyford Down or Oxleas Wood for example. It is time that the concept was extended to cover planning as a whole, and a good place to start would be with the presumption in favour of suburban planning.

There is little point in dwelling too long on the appropriateness, or otherwise, of low density monoculture suburban-style housing for large or small developments in the countryside. Nor, indeed, is it worth dwelling on its visual impact, for it speaks for itself. The Urban Villages Group report pub-lished recently argued strongly enough against the soullessness of such developments, putting forward instead a rather different approach based on higher densities and mixed uses. One cannot, indeed, avoid commenting on the extraordinary environmental wastefulness of this sort of development. It is wasteful in land because of the low density of the housing (particularly when it comes to single-storey bungalows) and the excessive space which has to be given over to roads and roundabouts. There are also many examples of the curious habit of building endless detached houses cheek by jowl as if to maximise the quantity of building materials re-quired. This also applies to the wastage of energy, given the unnecessary extra heating requirements of all those detached houses and bungalows which would be minimised if they were terraces. This added to the fact that such housing presupposes a life that revolves around the motor car. An environ-mental audit which balanced the demands of the road engineer against the use of resources required (including, of course, the effect on the local environ-ment) and the visual impact his demands entail might have a dramatic effect on the way we build.

My primary objection to suburban planning lies in its inappropriateness in a village context. Villages are infinitely varied in form depending on their history and geography, sometimes nucleated, sometimes essentially ribbon developments, sometimes based around a large village green, sometimes little more than a handful of hamlets scattered evenly through the countryside. The suburban cul-de-sac, however, which is the standard response of planners and developers, offers a single pattern of building of which only one thing is certain: you never find it in a traditional village.

There seems to be a strange belief that because villages are set in the countryside, surrounded by all that open space, new developments should be kept to a low density. As I have just made clear the very variety of village types makes it difficult to generalise, but most villages are characterised by fairly high densities. After all, land has always been precious. The most common village housing type is not the detached house but the terrace, mixed with a variety of pairs of houses and individual houses. The result is a relatively random mix of house types and densities in direct contrast to the even suburban layout with its identically sized houses repeated at regular intervals, each set in the middle of their small plot of land.

There is no reason why traditional patterns of development cannot be followed today. As a contrast to the suburban cul-de-sac one can consider a proposed development in the Lincolnshire village of Aubourn which has just been given planning consent. The proposal, by the architect Murray John, is for a comprehensive redevelopment of the centre of the village partly on the site of an existing farm and organised around a new village green, to be spread over several years. The development includes a terrace of three houses looking onto the green, another of four houses across the road, three pairs of houses, five detached houses and some sheltered housing. It should be a very successful addition because it follows and develops existing features of the village using traditional groupings and does not try to impose a predetermined but alien plan form.

Much thought has gone into Aubourn and similar schemes, of which the Poundbury extension to Dorchester is the most sophisticated, as to how cars can be incorporated into more traditional village layouts. Are those bland serpentine roads really necessary; do junctions need to be quite as splayed out; and are garages essential? After all, it is a common fate for them to be turned into workshops. If they are needed can they not be integrated more successfully with the houses, or modelled on the sort of ancillary buildings traditionally found around larger village houses? Malcolm Tempest has successfully taken this approach at North Stainley near Ripon in North Yorkshire. Often the answer lies in

grouping the carparking behind the houses, as long as this is carefully landscaped, and groups of garages set behind houses can often be organised to considerable architectural effect. Subsidiary buildings and activities such as wash houses, workshops, agricultural buildings, gardens and orchards have always been placed at the back of the house, and carparking and garages are no more than the modern equivalent of this. Above all, it is important to remember that it is the house which should be dominant. Moreover, this arrangement allows houses to open directly onto the street or to be set behind front gardens which not only gives friendlier and more attractive aspects but is traditional in most villages. Research into how the car can be mastered is among the most exciting current developments in planning, but calls for imagination on the part of the developer and his architect and flexibility from the Highways Engineer.

An important feature of both the Aubourn and North Stainley developments is the way that the new housing is integrated into the village rather than left as a detached unit. Indeed, in both cases, thanks to their new greens, the developments have become central parts of the village. This is important visually, but it is even more important socially. The great weakness of the massive wave of rural council house building which followed the last war was the way that it was nearly always arranged in mini-estates on the outskirts of the village. This had the effect of creating ghettos which failed to integrate with the village as a whole. The same danger is all too obvious in the isolated cul-de-sacs which are the product of the 80s.

Many of the ideas that lie behind the Aubourn scheme can also be found at Thicket Mead on the edge of Midsomer Norton in Avon, a proposed development of 110 houses designed by Robert Adam for the Duchy of Cornwall. In particular, both schemes deliberately mix different social types of housing – including a fair proportion of affordable housing. One of the strengths of the traditional village is the social integration of its housing, thanks to the way terraces, pairs of houses and individual houses are intermingled, each appealing to different social groups and income brackets. By contrast, uniform suburban cul-de-sacs, like post-war village council housing, isolate one social group from another. Moreover, because of the required low densities and the desire for developers to maximise their profits, an unbalanced percentage of new housing tends to be large 'executive' houses. This is one reason why such developments appear alien in a village where large houses have always been relatively scarce and certainly not arranged in groups of eight or ten together. One can, anyway, question the

Stephen Mattick, new house at Horseheath, Cambs

GM Saunders Designs Ltd Architects, White Cat Cottages, Horsington, Somerset

Willy Harbinson of the Percy Thomas Partnership, housing in Luccombe, Somerset

need for all these large houses, when many of the surveys quoted by house builders justifying their calls for new housing show that most new households which will be created in the coming decades will be one and two person households – for which terrace housing is ideal.

But the problems caused by the rash of new village housing in the 1980s was not simply a product of unsympathetic suburban planning, it was also a question of scale. Given time, villages can accommodate a considerable amount of development, but not if that development happens too quickly. This is true both socially and visually. Too many newcomers are hard to absorb in one go, while houses also take time to settle into a landscape, planting being particularly important. Of course there are great attractions to the developer in building a large number of houses on one site in a short period, above all economies in management time. It costs much the same in professional fees to sort out planning, highways and drainage for a development of three houses as it does for 20. No wonder developers prefer to build in large numbers. But 20 – or probably 50 or 100 – new houses at one time is far more than any village has ever known in one go and may cause a fatal case of indigestion. Nor should one forget that there are powerful forces behind large developments. It is worth the developers' while to take a major scheme to appeal when they may be able to railroad it through, but a small developer will not have the resources. These pressures must be resisted and new developments carefully phased if they are to be beneficial.

If, then, there is to be development, where should the houses go? Today firm village lines are increasingly being drawn beyond which new building is not permitted. As a method of control this has much to be said in its favour. Above all it protects the countryside from unnecessary development. But the counter effect is that it encourages infill in the village. Sensitively done and provided that the quality of the design matches the surrounding houses, infill can be a good thing. It works particularly well where there is an obvious gap in a village plan which is often the site of a lost house. But the danger of infill is that it ignores the importance of the open spaces – whether gardens, fields or orchards – to the appearance of a village. The attractiveness of a village derives partly from the beauty of its setting and the elegance of its houses but largely from the way that fields often push right to its centre. However, many villages in the south of England are now so heavily infilled that they resemble nothing so much as Alsatian geese fit only for foie gras. The other difficulty with firm village lines is that they are unhistorical. Insensitively drawn and controlled

they may freeze a village. Perhaps what is needed is for the line to be revised every ten years, allowing a small amount of controlled growth.

All this talk of planning presupposes that there are architects capable of designing houses fit for these sensitive situations. Drive round most of south-east England and you would be right to wonder, but there are exceptions, the work of architects who, given the chance, could be much more productive.

One of the great tragedies of Modernist architecture was the way that it divorced the architectural profession from rural housing design and, to an unfortunate degree, from speculative housing as a whole. In the 18th, 19th and early 20th centuries numerous leading architects designed village housing – one need only think of Robert Adam at Lowtherville, John Carr at Harewood, William Butterfield at Baldersby and George Devey at Penshurst. Perhaps more importantly, village housing was a staple part of the diet of innumerable unassuming but competent country architects. The basis of Modernism lay in breaking the link between the architect and architectural tradition and, as good rural housing design depends on a thorough knowledge of that tradition, and in particular the local vernacular, together with respect for context, this left a vacuum which has never been effectively filled. Most volume housebuilders do not use architects. Numerous local developers are little better. The result has been the acceptance all over the country of standard housing types which owe little or nothing to traditional village houses, the only nod to the locality perhaps being in the materials. The last ten years have seen a reviving interest among architects in the problem of village housing. I do not think it is a coincidence that this revival has followed the collapse of Modernism as an unchallenged approach to architecture. Architects are no longer embarrassed to be interested in tradition and context. Nor is it surprising that many of these architects, although inevitably trained as Modernists, have considerable experience in conservation, and have therefore developed their knowledge of traditional skills, forms and materials. They are nearly all local architects, and sadly their work has largely been ignored by the architectural press.

I have mentioned the work of Murray John, Robert Adam (based in Winchester) and Malcolm Tempest (based at Leyburn in Yorkshire). And there are many more architects whose work deserves attention. Among them are: Grahame Saunders of Bridport for his cottages in Horsington in Somerset and Michael Drury of Salisbury, for his in Bowerchalke, Wiltshire; Peterjohn Smyth of the Bristol office of the Percy Thomas Partnership, for his houses in Luccombe, Somerset; Hugh King of

CH Design, for Club Corner Cottages at Leigh, Dorset; Bertram and Fell of Bath for their cottages in Abbotsbury, Dorset; and Ken Morgan, based near Poole, for his cottages in Sturminster Marshall, Dorset; Stephen Langer in Kent; Francis Johnson and Partners in Yorkshire; Stephen Hawkins in Dorset; Alf Trewin in Devon, and there are doubtless many others whom I have yet to discover.

The fact that nearly all of these are local architects is very important. You can only design sympathetic new houses in a village if you know the local vernacular intimately and if you have made a good study of the site. I fear that all too many speculative houses are designed by people who never come within 100 miles of the village and are quite blind to the subtleties of local vernaculars. Of course, if planners are to play a positive role in promoting good rural design it is critically important that they have an equally thorough knowledge of the types of buildings to be found in their own areas.

Simplicity and attention to detail are the essence of good rural housing design. A close analysis of the few examples I have mentioned would provide many valuable lessons. It is all in the proportions, the relationship of window to wall, the pitch of the roof, the grouping of the individual houses, the way the fall of the land and the curve of the street are exploited. Decent chimneystacks make a big difference, as do porches. Windows, of course, are critical, both their size – and there is nothing less attractive in a village than a picture window which after all only stares straight into a neighbour's living room – and their design and colour. In additon to this, I have already discussed the need for houses to be set onto the street.

Appropriate materials are essential. Sometimes stone may be unavoidable, but render is almost always better than artificial stone. An attractive brick need be no more expensive than an ugly one, while much can be done with careful detailing and mixing of inexpensive materials. One major problem that needs to be overcome is the way that the excellent designs by an architect which gain outline planning permission can turn out to be a dreadful disappointment. This is because, in reality, the developer and builder – who no longer need the architect – use inappropriate materials and shoddy details in its execution.

None of this need be expensive. The great tragedy of most recent rural housing is that it costs little more to build well. Indeed it can easily be cheaper for, as I have shown, good village building is simple, economical building. Normally, however, the things that really matter, like design, are sacrificed to expensive extras which are thought to tempt the buyer, like fake half-timbering, bay windows and fitted kitchens. Given the premium attached to original village houses it is surprising that developers are not more anxious to emulate them.

Most of the examples I have looked at so far are relatively cheap buildings. They have to be because the majority fall into the category of social housing, built for rent or shared equity ownership. There must be something ironic about the fact that much of the best recent rural housing has been commissioned not by rich clients but by impoverished housing associations of which the Sutton (Hastoe) Housing Association stands out for its real commitment to architectural design. This is not chance, but the result of government relaxation of planning restrictions which allowed new social housing on sites – whether particularly sensitive ones on the centre of the village, or ones outside the village line – where speculative housing would not have been allowed. Such consents have, however, only been granted where the quality of the design matched that of the site. Housing associations were forced to employ good architects in order to get consents and the planners were firm in ensuring the high quality of the designs. Here lies the proof that a middle way is possible in rural housing design; that architects and developers – in this case the housing associations – under the guidance of the planners can produce sympathetic new village architecture. It is particularly sad, therefore, to discover that the ever-tightening financial constraints of the Housing Corporation have meant that many housing associations are abandoning this experiment just when it has proved to be so successful.

On their own, it is true, planners can do little. Without good architects, intelligent clients – whether developers, landowners or private individuals – and skilled builders nothing of quality can be achieved. But it is the planners who set the ground rules within which everyone else must work and who ultimately determine what can and cannot be built. Excepting, of course, when the Secretary of State intervenes, and one cannot avoid the fact that one reason why so much dross was allowed in the 80s was for fear that the developer would go to appeal and win, leaving the planners with no influence over the form of the development. Good rural housing design will never be anything more than exceptional if the government is not prepared to support the planners in their battle to achieve it.

The *ghetto-isation* of the countryside, the creation of unchanging islands of beauty in seas of mediocrity, cannot be a good thing. We only accept it because we assume that any new development must be for the worse. The skills and knowledge do exist to prove that there can be a middle way in rural housing if only we pay greater attention to design.

Michael Drury, village housing, Bowerchalke, Wilts

Ken Morgan, Abbotsbury Glebe, Dorset

DEMETRI PORPHYRIOS
REMARKS ON THE EC GREEN PAPER

The agenda on urbanism and architecture masterminded by the CIAM in the 20s and 30s was so successfully presented as a transfer of power to 'all people' that virtually no one, including the rank and file of CIAM, had any inkling of the physical and human devastation they were instituting.

The ideological *putsch* of Modernist planning (carried out under the pretext of scientific urbanism) requires emphasis because of the entrenched view that Modernist planning rose to power in the wake of an explosion of popular disatisfaction with the traditional city. That was never the case. Even Rayner Banham was quick to realise that 'this generality which gives the Athens Charter its air of universal applicability conceals a very narrow conception of both architecture and town planning and committed CIAM uneqivocally to rigid functional zoning of city plans with green belts between the areas reserved to the different functions ... At a distance of 30 years we recognise this as merely the expression of an aesthetic preference but at the time it had the power of a Mosaic commandment and effectively paralysed research . . . '

What is the origin, therefore, of the myth that Modernist planning is 'scientific, progressive and egalitarian'; when on the contrary, all empirical evidence points to its destructiveness of both the city and the countryside.

The answer may lie partly in psychology: most people find it natural to assume that what affects millions must have been willed by millions.

However, the principal reason for the legend of a populist Modernist urbanism is to be found in the requirements of the Modernist Party. CIAM could justify its authority neither by tradition nor by a popular mandate. To justify their authority, therefore, they claimed the mandate of history which they maintained had chosen them to usher in the final phase in urban evolution: that of a 'scientific, progressive and egalitarian' society.

Language was deliberately distorted: the word scientific was introduced as a guarantee for error-proof decisions; the word progressive was used to discredit human sentiment and historical wisdom as anachronistic and backward-looking; the word 'egalitarian' was intended as a promise for the total commodification of both urban and agrarian land. Since then, however, the Modernist regime has become less and less credible. Marked by self-deceptions, breaks and retreats, its ideologues have ultimately come to regret their planning strategies.

First, they renounced the Corbusian model of the Radiant City, adopting instead the low-rise mixed use model of the traditional city. Then they regretted suburbia as well as the monofunctional sectors of 'Living, Working, Recreation, Transportation and Historic Buildings' that CIAM had celebrated together with the senseless traffic engineering that such zoning policies required. Recently, they have come to realise that cities and the countryside are two sides of the same coin and that a balance between the two must be established once again.

However, the destruction of open countryside by indiscriminate sprawl, office parks, megastructural shopping malls and theme developments continues. The actual and potential environmental cost in senseless traffic engineering is immense. And yet, it is still only a potential.

A number of individuals have already drawn attention to the potential disaster that would follow from the destruction of the open countryside. Many civic bodies have raised the public's awareness and support to similar environmental issues. But until politicians are made to renounce the narrow commercialism that undermines the balance between our cities and countryside nothing significant will be achieved.

It is for that reason that the *Green Paper for the Urban Environment* must be greeted with enthusiasm and hope. It is a first step towards addressing the balance between urbanisation and the countryside. I must stress here that though the Commission of the European Communities is taking up the problems of the urban environment, the ensuing implications for safeguarding against the destruction of the countryside are immense. Once again, it is important to recognise that cities and the countryside are two sides of the same coin.

It is fortunate that at last the country/city debate has reached the EC Commission. The Commission must now show statesmanship in dealing with legislation.

For our part we must recognise that the debate between the Traditional City and Modernist planning is *not* about stylistics. It is rather the wider question of the extent to which social and private institutions (and by extension individuals) should be committed to patterns of settlement which encourage urban life while safeguarding an unspoilt countryside. In other words, should modern societies continue to accept industrial degradation as a concomitant of modern life; or should we be allowed to choose for ourselves what is a worthwhile human life?

OPPOSITE: Demetri Porphyrios, Belvedere Village, Ascot

GREEN PAPER ON THE URBAN ENVIRONMENT
COMMISSION OF THE EUROPEAN COMMUNITIES

I THE FUTURE OF URBAN DEVELOPMENT
The Root Causes of Urban Degradation
Distribution and Consumption

The age of mass consumption has had a profound impact on the spatial organisation of the city. One such phenomenon is the large shopping mall at the far periphery, accessible only by car . . . Meanwhile, high-class shops take over the most picturesque parts of the old centre, depriving its inhabitants of shops for their daily needs. Other central areas are taken over by pedestrian zones, crammed with a narrow range of clothing and similar shops, which reduce variety and convenience for inhabitants and attract large amounts of traffic to surrounding parking garages.

There is thus a link between single-purpose public spaces and urban monoculture generally: the pedestrian area creates shopping precincts; the urban motorway, office ghettos. The equilibrium resulting from many uses and many modes of transport co-existing is lost.

Hotels, Restaurants and Housing

Increasingly, the centres are inhabited by three groups: older people with modest means, immigrants and young professionals, well-off and without children, benefitting from private or public urban restoration in what is known as 'gentrification'.

The neighbourhoods surrounding the centre, built in the second half of the 19th century, show a greater diversity of age and social groups. They are, however, assailed by traffic passing to the centre, and by encroachments from office development.

Further on the periphery, housing estates often represent extremes of monoculture, both as regards the social status of their inhabitants and the absence of multiple urban services and activities.

While the growth of these dormitory towns can in part be explained as a response by public authorities to a pressing need, they also follow a doctrinaire view developed before World War I which saw the 'garden city' as an ideal. This attempt to provide the city's inhabitants with air, quiet and space has unfortunately too often resulted in urban sprawl and further decentralisation.

The price is the need for a massive transport infrastructure whose main effects are felt by districts closer to the centre; and, for the individual, long travelling time . . .

These effects have contributed to create a movement of 'return to the city' . . . The demand for attractive urban housing suitable for families is beginning to be met by a still often experimental supply of roads with traffic restrictions where children can play and adults mingle, small but well-planted parks and play areas, replanted courtyards, roof gardens etc.

These experiments show that the 'mixing' of urban uses – of living, moving, working – is possible and, increasingly, necessary. *This new concept takes as its model the old, traditional life of the European city, stressing density, multiple use, social and cultural diversity.* Different social, professional and age groups living together also create the basis for a civil coexistence . . .

However, the housing estates of the periphery, increasingly suffering from vandalism and crime provoked by limited occupational choice, monotony and isolation also have to be urbanised in this new-old pattern: by creating greater heterogeneity, centres of greater density, life, and variety of uses.

Communication and Mobility

Some futurologists have concluded that modern communications technology could allow those now living and working in congested cities to disperse throughout the country. Everything argues against such a vision for all but a few independent professionals: the sheer number of people relative to the land available, the destruction of the environment involved, the implied waste of existing urban infrastructure.

Personal mobility thus remains an essential – indeed, the essential – attribute of the city. As argued above, spatial separation dictated by functionalist doctrine leaves, in the absence of effective public transport networks, little alternative to the motor car . . .

Outright prohibition of the car is rarely the answer . . . it may accelerate the monofunctional quality of the centre. It may force detours which increase overall traffic and hence pollution, or shift the problem of parking to the edge of the protected centre.

Generally, the objective must be to make the car an option rather than a necessity . . . The multifunctional, creative city, which is also the more livable city, is the one that pollutes the least. In turn, by limiting the car's contribution to noise, unsafe streets and air pollution, the city's attractions can grow and its economic, social, and cultural potential be realised.

Concretely, this leads to three convergent orientations:
– *avoid strict zoning in favour of mixed uses of urban*

space, favouring in particular housing in inner city areas
– *defend the architectural heritage against the uniform banality of the international style*, respecting rather than imitating the old
– *avoid escaping the problems of the city by extending its periphery: solve its problems within existing boundaries*

II TOWARDS A COMMUNITY STRATEGY FOR THE URBAN ENVIRONMENT
Targets for Urban Environmental Improvement

The primary objectives of urban environmental policy and management are the creation, or re-creation, of towns and cities which provide an attractive environment for their inhabitants, and the reduction of the city's contribution to global pollution. However utopian this may appear, it is one which meets today's concerns and tomorrow's responsibilities.

The analysis of the previous section traces urban environmental problems primarily to two factors.

The first of these is the uncontrolled pressure placed on the environment by many of the activities which are concentrated in the cities.

The second – and not unrelated – is the spatial arrangement of our urban areas. In the past few decades, planning philosophy and development practice have radically altered the organisation of towns, in many cases giving rise to an almost clinical separation of land uses. This has required urban populations greatly to increase their mobility, and thus their reliance on motor vehicles in general and private transport in particular.

This has in turn led to the development of extensive suburban residential areas which are economically difficult to service by public transport. The environmental implications of such spatial reorganisation of our cities may be seen in terms of:
– adverse effects on specific areas within towns: congested or decaying city centres; peripheries turned into dumping grounds for land uses considered undesirable for the city – waste tips, industry, social housing
– generally high levels of air and noise pollution, caused in part by the mobility imposed by spatial differentiation

Moreover, this pollution spills over into the country and the global environment. By their very concentration, cities are major contributors to acid rain and – via CO_2 emissions – to the greenhouse effect. Higher smoke-stacks are thus not the answer.

Areas of Action, Urban Planning
Encouraging greater diversity, avoiding urban sprawl

The strict zoning policies of the past decades which have led to the separation of land use and the subsequent development of extensive residential suburbs *have in turn stimulated commuter traffic, which is at the heart of many of the environmental problems currently facing urban areas.*

We therefore need a fundamental review of the princi-
ples on which town planning has been based. *Strategies which emphasise mixed use and denser development are more likely to result in people living close to work places and the services they require for everyday life.* The car can then become an option rather than a necessity.

Redeveloping Urban Wastelands

The many tracts of abandoned land, disused industrial sites, railway sidings, docks and military facilities in urban areas offer valuable opportunities for redevelopment – saving existing recreational and open space within cities and their outskirts from encroachment by development. Many cities have already accepted this priority in their planning strategies. However, the problems posed by contaminated land and complex ownership patterns are such that it will often require a firm lead from public authorities.

Revitalising Existing City Areas

Revitalising existing housing areas within the city is also important … Quality of life can be dramatically improved by carrying out environmental improvements and, specifically, by reducing the noise and pollution from traffic. This requires local strategies that give priority to the needs of pedestrians and inhabitants rather than to drivers passing through an area. Such environmental improvements may well provide the impetus for private investment in improvement of housing stock.

The need for revitalisation is not restricted to areas within the city. Many urban peripheral housing estates … are showing symptoms of urban decline more traditionally associated with rundown inner-city areas. In London and Marseille, the Commission is involved in pilot projects aimed at improving economic and social development in such areas. The problems experienced by their inhabitants are often aggravated by their physical isolation from the economic and cultural life of the city.

Expanding the uses and activities of these areas, and thus the opportunities available to their residents, is part of a strategy aimed at integrating these housing estates into the city, and improving their environment and the quality of life of their inhabitants.

Urban Design

Urban environmental quality is as much a product of building design as of spatial differentiation. *Protecting the visual quality and historical identity of our cities thus requires attention not only to the protection of historical buildings but also to the design of new buildings being inserted into the urban fabric.* Urban planning should therefore incorporate this third dimension, encouraging architectural innovation but *ensuring that new buildings are compatible with existing urban character* and do not destroy or render useless the city's open spaces.

Extracts selected and italicised by Demetri Porphyrios

41

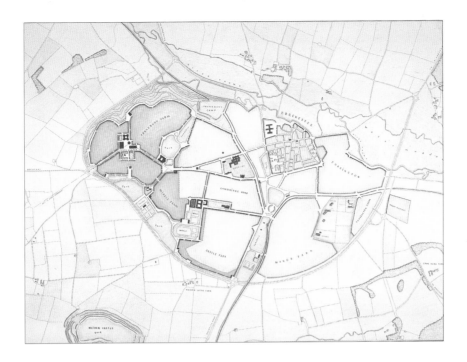

LEON KRIER
POUNDBURY
Dorset

Each quarter of Poundbury is a small town with local functions located in the central local squares and high streets which connect them with the civic centres around Castlefields school and Poundbury farm. The latter will contain leisure, cultural, education and administrative facilities which are of interest and use to all of Dorchester and to the county of Dorset.

Located at the heart of Middle Farm Quarter, Krier's tower is designed as a focal point for the neighbourhood and a landmark for the entire proposal.

Phase one of Poundbury is a mixed development which consists of shops, offices, workshops and public buildings as well as approximately 250 houses and flats. Krier's planning reflects the layout of traditional Dorset towns. The intention is that the buildings should be in the Dorset vernacular, and make full use of the traditional materials of that area.

The Duchy of Cornwall intends to procure the construction of roads and infrastructure, and to sell single plots or groups of plots to individuals, house-builders and developers for the construction of buildings. The plots for buildings of special importance within the townscape will be sold with scheme designs prepared by architects who have been commissioned by the Duchy of Cornwall.

These buildings are intended to set high standards which others should strive to match. It is intended that other buildings should be designed and constructed to the requirements of a code. The aim of the code is to communicate the intended character of the scheme and ensure conformity to the masterplan and a consistently high quality of design and construction, without stifling creativity and spontaneity.

The Duchy wishes to provide a development which is environmentally better than conventional designs. All houses will be environmentally assessed, using the Building Research Establishment Environmental Assessment Method. The scheme uses independent assessors to evaluate the environmental effects of the building at the design stage. The issues included affect the global, local and indoor environment, and credits will be given for design features which are better than normal practice and minimum Building Regulation requirements.

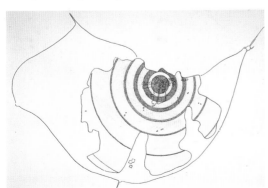
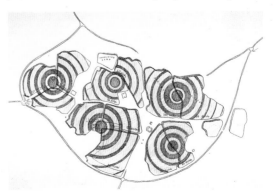

OPPOSITE: STREET PERSPECTIVE; *ABOVE*: PLAN OF NEW PROPOSALS; *BELOW*: EXISTING ANTI-URBAN PATTERN AND PROPOSED TOWN OF NEIGHBOURHOODS

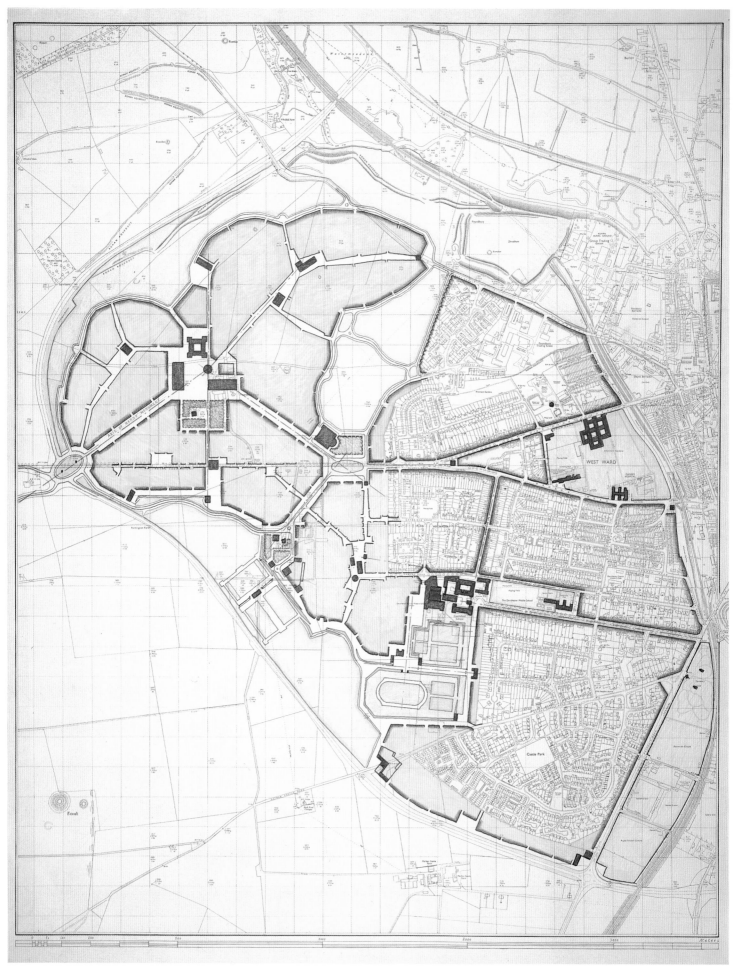

PLAN SHOWING BOUNDARIES OF EXISTING AND NEW URBAN QUARTERS

44

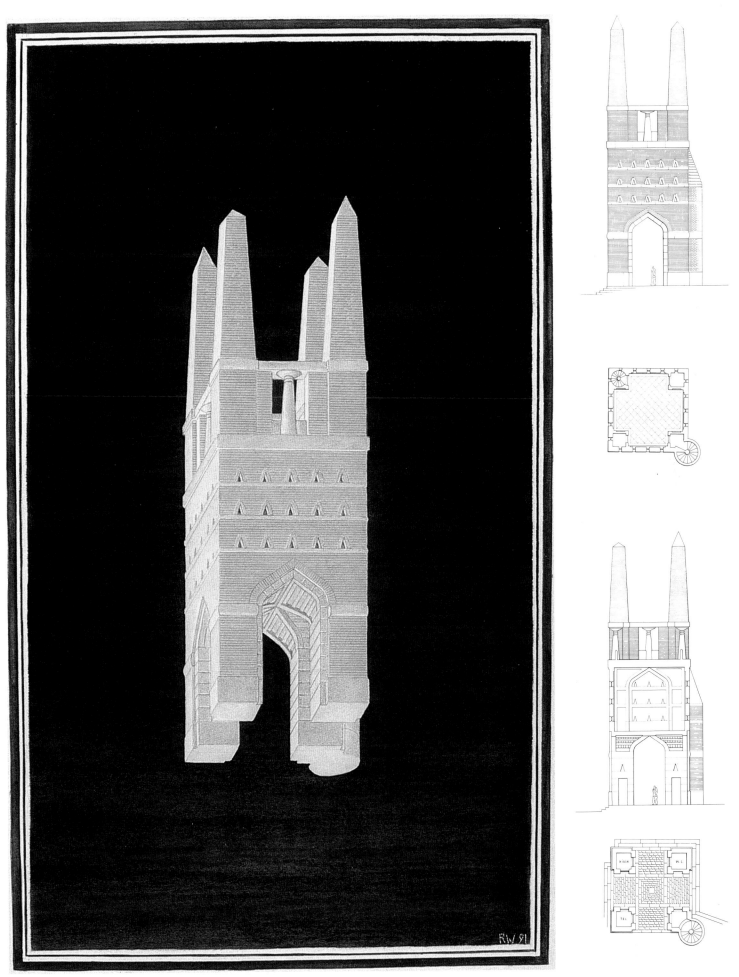

ABOVE: AXONOMETRIC OF TOWER; *RIGHT, ABOVE TO BELOW*: TOWER ELEVATION; FLOOR PLAN OF ASSEMBLY ROOM; TOWER SECTION; GROUND FLOOR PLAN

45

AERIAL PERSPECTIVE OF POUNDBURY

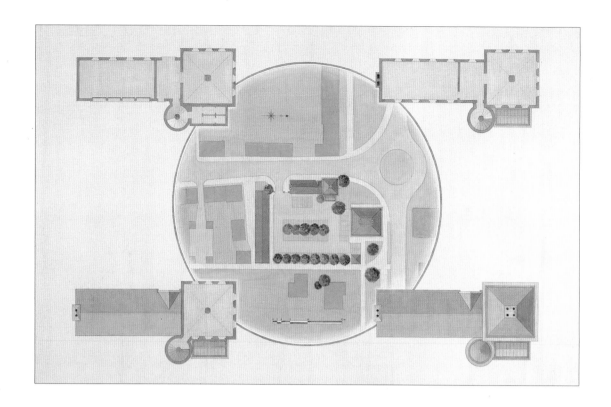

DEMETRI PORPHYRIOS
WORKSHOP AND OFFICES
Poundbury

The overall masterplan of the Poundbury development combines housing and work places as well as social and public facilities in the form of a traditional town. The workshop and office buildings are located at one of the most prominent approaches into the new development and, together with the buildings across the street, they act as a gateway into the town. The boundaries were established by the masterplan.

In this scheme, which makes use of local stone and slates, the main entrance to the offices is through a vaulted passage which at the same time connects the street with the court at the rear. The workshops are entered directly from the court. A separate three-storey building houses the offices. In addition to its perimeter bearing walls this building has a central pier which doubles both as structure and mechanical duct. The two

buildings are connected by the staircase tower. Further workshops define the boundaries of the site. The buildings are constructed in load-bearing masonry walls with ashlar stone or range walling externally. They have rough cut stone lintels for openings and local stone slates for the roofs.

This is an architecture that derives from the constructional logic of its natural materials and where the building fabric improves with age and weathering. It is an architecture of straightforward, solid, durable and beautiful buildings.

Working with the local vernacular one constantly marvels at the way in which complex problems are addressed with an ingenious simplicity. Vernacular building has manifold duties to perform but it allows no pure artifice to interfere with the law of sound construction and practical provision.

ABOVE: SITE AND FLOOR PLANS; *BELOW*: ELEVATION OF EAST FRONT

48

JOHN SIMPSON
THE MARKET BUILDING
Poundbury

Together with the tower by Leon Krier, the market building is one of two major public buildings in the main square of the Duchy of Cornwall's Poundbury development. The building is designed to provide a covered market area at ground level as part of the main square with a coffee house at one end. Upstairs it contains a public hall which runs the whole length of the building and is designed very much in the nature of an English village hall. It occupies a key position in the overall design and is particularly important to the views looking down the various streets leading towards the square and together with the tower is prominent in the skyline of the development.

The architecture, the general arrangement and the scale of the market building was designed to respond to its position and was deliberately intended to be of a robust and solid character.

It has therefore been designed to stand out, together with the tower, from the surrounding ordinary brick buildings by appearing to be of a much more substantial nature. Large irregular stone blocks are used for quoins which sit high on a solid stone plinth. Stone is also used for dressings, window surrounds, sills, carved finials, columns and archivolts. Grey delibole slate is used on the roof and is laid in diminishing courses. The main building material, however, is brick applied with a rough stucco render which is then painted. All the timber work, the windows and doors are painted in a deep bottle green. The paving at ground level is large York stone slabs. A series of large oak beams are a feature of the ceiling at ground level and internally the roof of the hall is all in timber with a series of massive trusses left entirely visible.

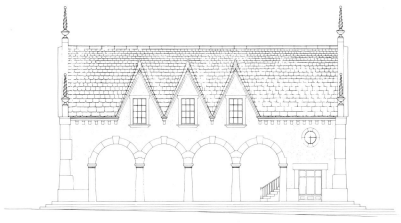

ABOVE: PERSPECTIVE VIEW; *BELOW*: ELEVATION

DEMETRI PORPHYRIOS
BELVEDERE VILLAGE
Ascot

Set in the Surrey landscape close to Ascot, this village unfolds around three main spaces: the farm, the residential and the stable courtyards. These provide spatial unity and accommodation for the various aspects of the brief. Of dissimilar type and scale they connect to form a chain of interrelated spaces.

A number of cottages together with the estate office are grouped to form the residential court. This is connected to the farm court by two short flights of steps and can be entered directly from the lane. The emphasis here is on the informal nature of villages. The different cottages are related in scale and materials while their grouping emphasises the spatial enclosure of the court. Second-hand red Surrey and yellow London bricks are used with tiled roofs. The eaves and joinery details are similar throughout, although each cottage is given its individual character by the configuration of the plan and its overall massing. The lodge, by contrast, is a single-storey timber structure set into the forested land and its raised porch inflects towards a passage which leads to the stable yard.

The stable yard is situated to the east, close to the forested area. It is formed by a number of frontally arranged buildings, all with cobbled aprons before them. At the centre is a granite water trough with a canopy of mature trees. Most of the buildings in the yard are stables designed on a regular bay system. Some are single-storey whilst others have accommodation for the grooms above, consisting of a timber-framed structure with a continuous balcony. The carriage house is a

further development of the stable type, comprising a large hall with various appendages for tack rooms and stores to the rear and with three large gabled doors at the front. Above each door slatted timber screens light the hall. The Head Groom's cottage is essentially a small tower with ancillary rooms while the hay barn is a single but monumental tetrapylon.

The existing pond has been extended to form a boundary that separates the farm court from the lane and the land beyond. The court is reached across a new stone bridge. Facing the bridgehead is the main barn which is intended for a variety of public functions. A dovecote tower marks the urban ensemble of the whole village and shows the way to the route up towards the stable court. Opposite the barn and overlooking the pond stands the hall. Raised on a plinth above the court and supported by buttressed walls to the west, the hall displays its hierarchical importance by the refinement of its details and materials. The building is organised around a central hall. Its oak roof and fireplace are variations on the theme encountered in the main barn and from the balcony overlooking the pond distant views of the open landscape can be enjoyed. The farm court has the urbanity of a village square and at its centre there is an ancient well which, together with the subtle change of levels and the newly planted lime trees, provides a focus to the court and gives it an intimate scale.

OPPOSITE: Stables and Head Groom's cottage; ABOVE: Dovecote

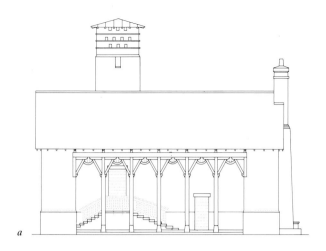

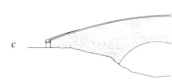

a

b

c

f

h

j

k

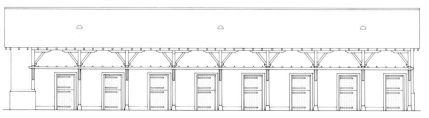

a MAIN BARN; *b* FIELD GATE; *c* BRIDGEHEAD; *d* LODGE; *E* HALL; *f* GARDENER'S COTTAGE; *g* CARRIAGE HOUSE; *h* FARMER'S COTTAGE; *i* ESTATE OFFIC

d

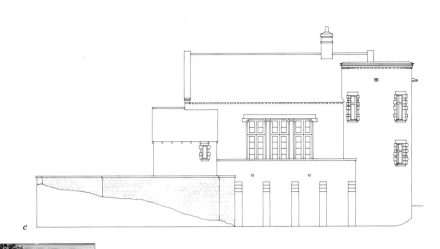

e

g

i

m

AD GROOM'S COTTAGE; *k* STABLES; *l* STABLES AND GROOMS' ACCOMMODATION; *m* HAY BARN; *CENTRE*: MODEL OF THE SCHEME; *OVERLEAF*: GENERAL VIEW

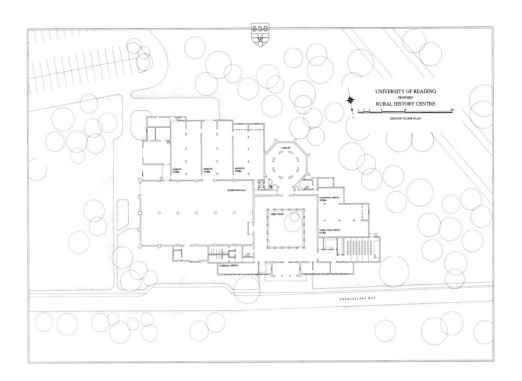

RURAL HISTORY CENTRE
Reading University

The winning scheme for the provision of a permanent buiding to house the Rural History Centre, the new building is located on Chancellors Way, at the main entrance to the University campus against the backdrop of playing fields and mature woodland. The massing of the building is broken up so that full advantage is taken of the foreshortened as well as the distant views offered by the site. The main entrance is marked by a timber-roofed portico with flanking wings on either side. Upon entry one arrives at the very heart of the building: an open-air court surrounded by a five metre wide arcade. The various activities of the brief are organised around this central arcaded court. The lecture hall and seminar rooms are located near the main entrance, the academic staff's offices and study rooms on the first floor overlooking the court, and the archival stores and reserve collections on the ground floor.

To the south of the central court and on axis with the main entrance is the library. This is an octagonal room with a lofty reading room in the centre, support services in the ambulatory and open access shelving in the gallery above.

The exhibition gallery to the east of the central court is a great hall marked by a series of brick columns in the centre and engaged pilasters along the perimeter walls; all support- ing a roof comprising a number of truncated pyramids with skylit tops. An increased draught effect is created by a system of wind induced extraction which is enhanced by the shape of the pyramidal roofs in a manner similar to the traditional principle of passive ventilation found in oast houses.

In the design of the museum reference has been made to the brick architecture common in the Reading area and more generally to traditional materials. The building is constructed in load-bearing walls with red facing bricks externally. Copings, corbels, window and door surrounds and band courses are all in natural stone. Roofs are in timber and are finished in natural slates or lead.

OPPOSITE: PERSPECTIVE VIEW OF ENTRANCE FRONT; *ABOVE*: GROUND FLOOR PLAN; *BELOW*: SOUTH ELEVATION

ABOVE: VIEW OF ABBOTSBURY FROM ST CATHERINE'S CHAPEL BEFORE THE NEW PROPOSALS; *CENTRE*: PLAN OF ABBOTSBURY SHOWING THE NEW ADDITIONS; *BELOW*: AERIAL VIEW OF ABBOTSBURY BEFORE THE NEW PROPOSALS

BERTRAM & FELL
ABBOTSBURY VILLAGE PLAN

The Abbotsbury Estate has been owned by one family for centuries. In the early 1970s most of the houses were in poor repair, needing a huge investment to upgrade them while yielding very little income in return. The owner commissioned a report from the architects William Bertram and Fell. In 1973 they produced 'An Appreciation of Abbotsbury' which, together with its companion document 'The Abbotsbury Village Plan' prepared jointly with the West Dorset District Council, formed the basis of the estate's management policy and the Local Authority's planning policy. The core of the plan was to finance the improvement of the existing housing stock by the sale on long leases of building plots for infill housing and redundant buildings, such as barns, for conversion into houses and workshops. By the use of long-leases the estate has been able to maintain control over the design and detailing of the new buildings and of alterations to the old. This control has been exercised through their consultant architects, William Bertram & Fell, who vet all architects' plans on their behalf. The future of this policy, however, is now at risk due to proposed changes in the law affecting leases.

The guidelines in the 'Appreciation' require architects to use the local vernacular with houses built of stone, roofed with thatch or slate, with small windows and traditional doors and with attention paid to established local details. Alien elements such as ornate sedgework on thatching and stained hardwood windows have been resisted. Within the village framework, the siting of the new houses in terraces built up against the roads, and the insistence that their scale and proportions mirror the original buildings has resulted in a seamless evolution.

Since 1973, over 20 new houses have been built and as many conversions and restorations on long leases carried out on the estate's property. These include a terrace of six houses designed by William Bertram & Fell for the Sutton Hastoe Housing Association in Back Street, a group of three cottages and a detached house designed by Clive Hawkins for the developer Michael Still. One of the earliest barn conversions was of Chapel Barn in Chapel Lane by William Bertram & Fell for Admiral Sir John Hamilton. The estate has also improved all its retained housing stock. In the last year, a group of 28 houses designed by Ken Morgan has been built by the Raglan Housing Association on glebe land outside the control of the estate, but it is encouraging to note that they have adhered to the design guidelines which have now become so well established in Abbotsbury.

ABOVE: NORTH-EAST VIEW OF ABBOTSBURY; *BELOW*: SUTTON HASTOE HOUSES IN BACK STREET

ABOVE: TERRACED HOUSES IN BACK STREET; *BELOW LEFT*: DETACHED HOUSE FROM REAR; *BELOW RIGHT*: REAR VIEW OF TERRACE

CLIVE HAWKINS
HOUSING IN ABBOTSBURY

In 1987 the project to design a small group of traditional stone cottages on a corner site in Back Street began. It was decided to build a terrace of three cottages on the site of an existing derelict stone building with a separate dwelling to be built at the rear for the client's own residence. Materials were chosen to fit in with the vernacular architecture of the area and were therefore natural ham stone, with water reed thatch. The style and position of windows reflected the local traditions and were of white painted softwood. Since the site was on rising ground, retaining walls had to be designed and built on land behind the terrace of cottages, and the rear cottage constructed on several levels. Building work was completed in 1991.

ABOVE: ELEVATION TO BLIND LANE; *BELOW*: VIEW OF COTTAGES FROM BACK STREET

ABOVE AND BELOW: VIEWS OF THE NEW BUILDINGS ON THE SQUARE

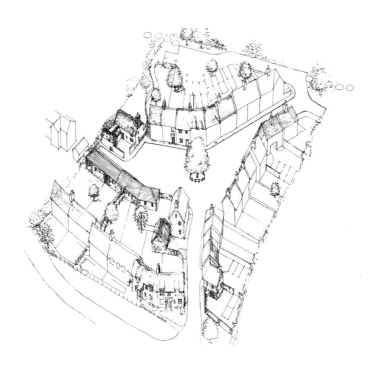

KEN MORGAN
ABBOTSBURY GLEBE

The rural housing crisis is very real for young families in West Dorset. There are too few homes in an area characterised by pretty villages set in glorious countryside close to an unspoilt coast. Planning policies revolve around Areas of Outstanding Natural Beauty, Heritage Coastlines, Conservation Areas and tightly drawn Village Envelopes. The Department of the Environment Circular 7/91 'Planning and Affordable Housing' encouraged Planners to allow exceptions to their normal policies 'in considering the release of small sites which would not otherwise be allocated for housing, within or adjoining existing villages.' Abbotsbury is a fine example of this policy. With the support of West Dorset council members, very conscious of their social responsibilities and their enlightened Planning Officer, David Oliver, a joint venture was devised whereby the Diocese sold their glebe land to Raglan Housing Association and a local builder, CG Fry and Son Ltd. Ken Morgan designed a layout of terraced cottages appropriate to Abbotsbury. These are of stone, with slate and thatched roofs, and are arranged in curving terraces tight to the back of footpaths around a simple tarmac 'square', relieved only by a single oak tree. The curving road alignment with cars parked by the front doors, where people want them, keeps down vehicle speeds. The space and ambience reproduce the essential quality of older and much loved country villages.

Twenty cottages are either rented or sold on an equity share basis by Raglan. Eight cottages are being sold on the open market with part of their value being used to subsidise the high cost of stone and thatch.

ABOVE: AXONOMETRIC OF ABBOTSBURY GLEBE; *BELOW*: VIEW OF ABBOTSBURY GLEBE (UNDER CONSTRUCTION)

Francis Johnson & Partners, Cricket Pavilion. *The cricket pavilion was commissioned to stand in the extensive grounds of a private house in North Yorkshire. Influenced by its parkland setting, the building is a timberframed structure clad in timber boarding with a paint finish*

JOHN ROBINS
PAVILION OVER THE SPRING
Gloucestershire

In a hidden valley, on the edge of dense woods in Gloucester-shire, this pavilion straddles the source of a magical spring. When the architect was given the commission it was to construct a building for garden tools which would at the same time adorn a meandering cress stream where dippers feed and the banks are choked with yellow mimulus. The four year drought ended and the spring abruptly burst from the hill-side.

Materials used were new and reused Cotswold stone with old stone roofing slates and lead flashings. The turreted form of the square building evokes dovecotes and the triangular openings are traditional in Cotswold barns and farm build-ings. The owners propose to stand candles in the niches either side of the door for fêtes champetres.

As the rains fell through the summer months, the water rose and the materials were transported down the river. The building will be completed in spring 1993.

ABOVE AND BELOW: VIEWS OF PAVILION

PERSPECTIVE

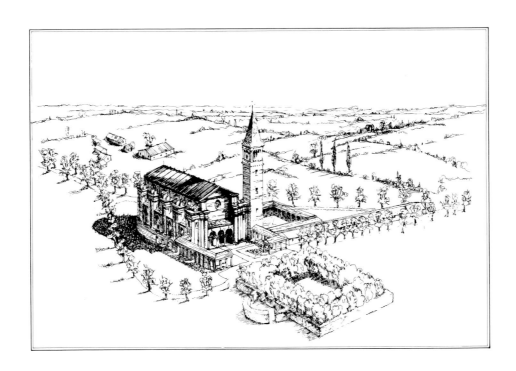

ALLAN GREENBERG
CHURCH OF THE IMMACULATE CONCEPTION
New Jersey

A new Roman Catholic church to be built in Clinton, New Jersey, adjacent to the existing church. The latter is a converted barn which will be used for a chapel, classrooms and offices. The bell tower is the locus of the plan and connects the new church and its formal entry court, via a cloister, to the chapel, classrooms and offices of the church.

The entry court frames the main entrance of the church and provides access to the chapel on one side and to a stair down to the ground floor community room on the other. The colonnade and its Tuscan Order become the minor order of the church. The church entrance is expressed by the enlarged scale of three arches and incorporates a 'Galilee' or covered entrance.

The new church's interior and exterior are articulated by a major order of paired pilasters which define square structural bays. The ceiling of the nave is an elliptical barrel vault and

the buttressing function of the bays is expressed by the exterior massing. Circular and rectangular fenestration distinguishes the two double-storey bays from the single-storey connecting bays. Arched openings occur at the connecting bays and are supported on the minor order of columns, the same as those of the entry court colonnade. They define ancillary spaces off the main sanctuary which are used for chapels, sacristy, choir, stairs and confessionals. Both interior and exterior are articulated by an A:B:A rhythm of structure and spaces. This rhythm changes to A:A:A in the semicircular apse behind the high altar where the pilasters become attached columns. The setting of the church is a large rural site. It is to have a cemetery, a Marian Shrine and a formal garden with the remainder of the site as a meadow. The garden will be used for church activities. The landscape is designed by the architect.

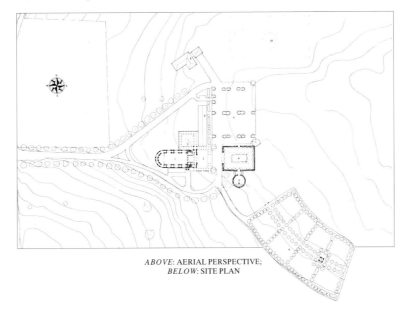

ABOVE: AERIAL PERSPECTIVE;
BELOW: SITE PLAN

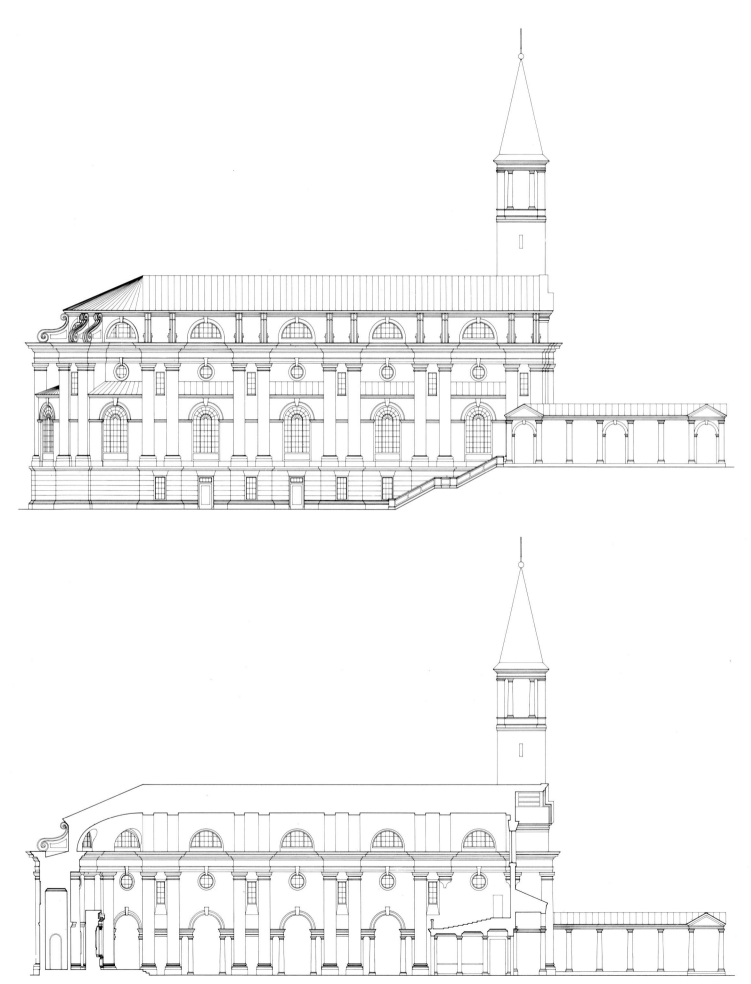

ABOVE: SOUTH ELEVATION; *BELOW*: LONGITUDINAL SECTION

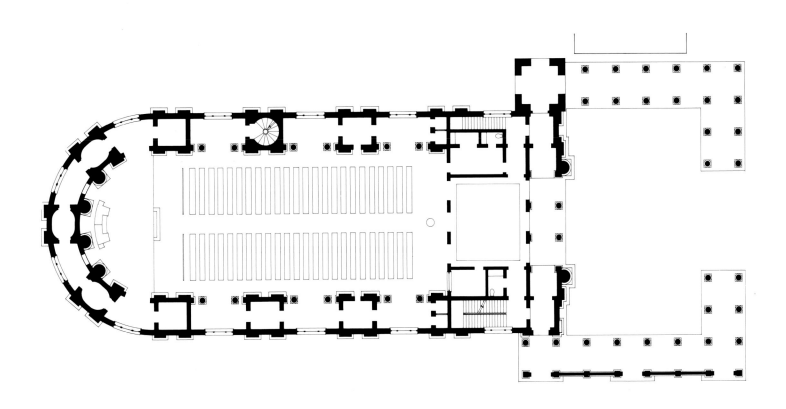

ABOVE LEFT: EAST ELEVATION; *RIGHT*: LATERAL SECTION; *BELOW*: FIRST FLOOR PLAN

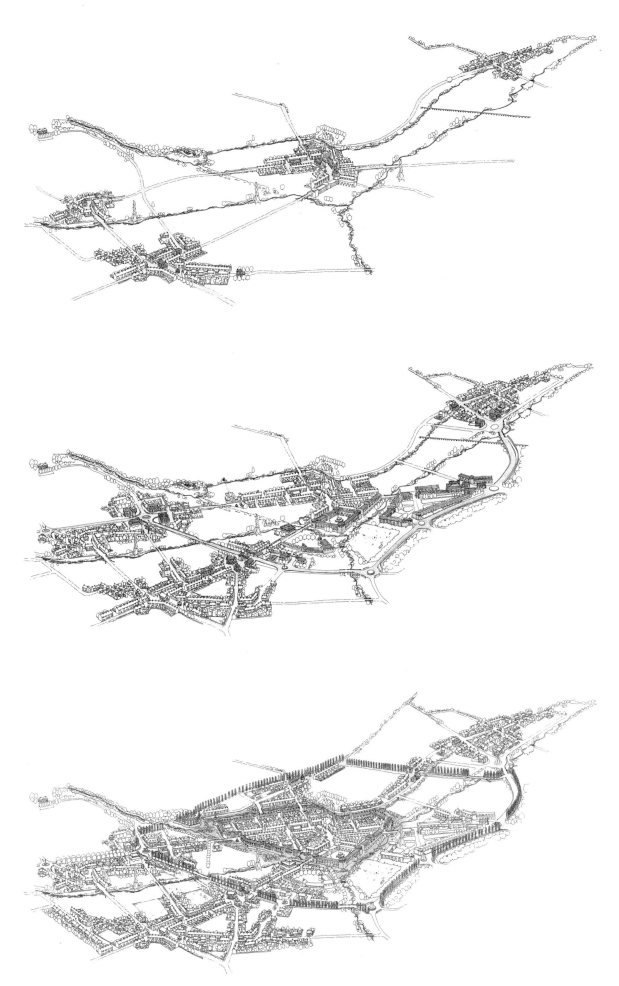

ABOVE: VILLAGE CENTRES; *CENTRE*: SECONDARY PUBLIC SPACES AND BUILDINGS; *BELOW*: ENTIRE DEVELOPMENT WITH LANDSCAPING FEATURES

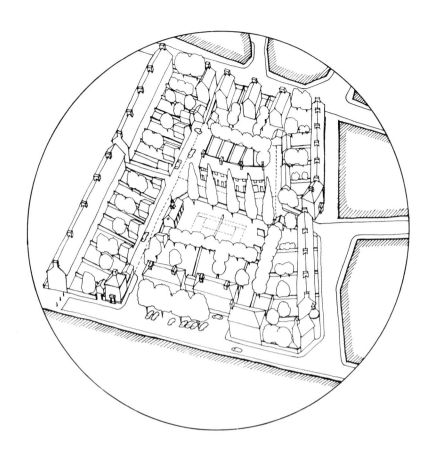

JOHN SIMPSON
COLDHARBOUR FARM DEVELOPMENT
Aylesbury

The Coldharbour Farm Development is a development covering roughly 200 acres of land on the periphery of the town of Aylesbury. It consists of 1,500 houses, half a million square feet of employment buildings and associated public buildings such as a church, village halls, shops, a school and a clinic.

The land belongs to the Ernest Cook Trust, an educational charity set up in the 1920s. The aim of the Trust has been to create a new place that has a coherent identity, character and a sense of community and is not just another collection of anonymous housing estates. In this respect the Trust commissioned a masterplan from John Simpson and Partners. Their approach has been to subdivide the site into a series of village centres based on an acceptable walking distance for the pedestrian. This allows every inhabitant to be no more than five minutes walk away from the centre. The object being to make it convenient and desirable to get about freely.

The major public spaces and associated public buildings are arranged around these centres. Secondary public spaces and their associated commercial and employment buildings are then arranged along the natural pedestrian routes but with additional easy access for vehicles and servicing. A main distributor road runs through the site as part of the overall highway network for Aylesbury and has been used to service these areas without creating unnecessary disruption by

running it along the natural boundary between the villages. It has therefore been treated as if it was devised to follow the line of an old boundary such as an old city wall with an elevated walk planted with fastigiate Hornbeam trees. These trees continue a circular walk around the site that follows the line of an existing high pressure water main, and a gas main over which it would otherwise be undesirable to build.

The site also has a series of small riverlets which are part of the local flood plain and these have been used as a feature creating a high density area which appears to be of an almost fortified nature at the heart of the site. The houses are laid out using blocks roughly 90 metres square. The new buildings are arranged along the edge of the blocks and define the new streets in the traditional manner leaving a hollow centre to each block that can then be used much like a traditional mews to provide for car parking and servicing away from the street.

The streets themselves are designed to accommodate highway and safety criteria for the motor car. Visibility lines, stopping distances and junction splays as well as car parking requirements are considered as part of the masterplan. These are incorporated without loss of urban character by ensuring that the layout is designed to keep traffic speeds low. Methods and standards for achieving this have been devised and agreed with Buckingham County Council Highway Engineers.

AERIAL PERSPECTIVE

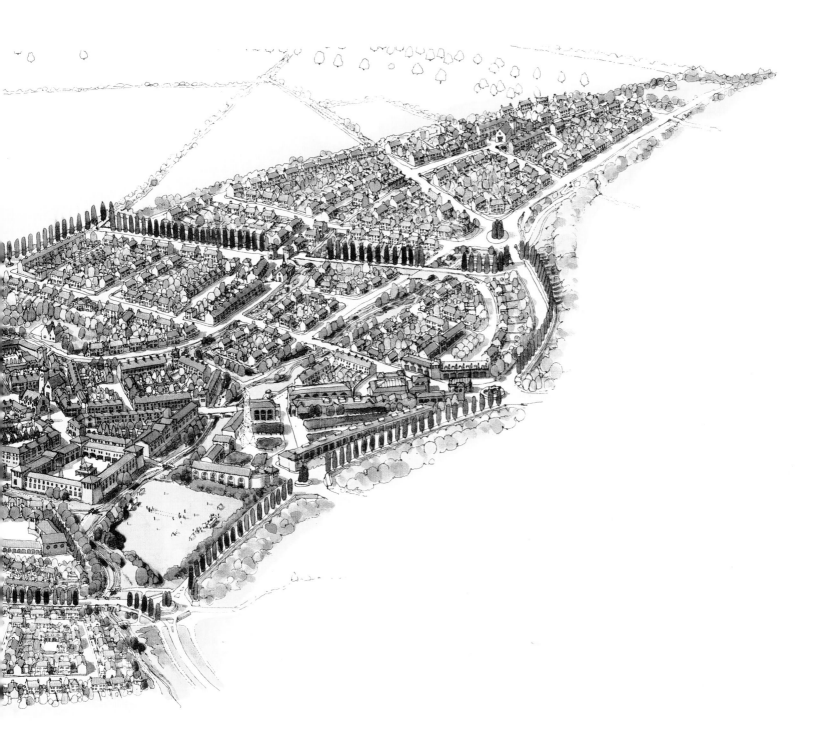

DRAWINGS OF STREET SCENES

ROBERT ADAM
NEW HOUSING IN A VILLAGE PLAN
Shepton Mallet

The development area of 37 acres is within easy walking distance of the centre of Shepton Mallet but is isolated by a park and a disused railway cutting. The 300 dwellings are incorporated in a scheme based on the village pattern and building types of the locality. A significant mixture of uses was precluded since a surplus of small commercial units exists in the area and shopping in the town centre was depressed. However, a new primary school and one shop provide a focal point. Future demands for small relatively inexpensive houses and social need housing have also been allowed for.

Building is centred on two internal open spaces: a green and a square linked by a street of high density housing. There are a series of secondary spaces and streets where densities and the character of the plan vary. The normal commercial principle of maximising each dwelling as a unit has been specifically avoided, the amenity of each building or group of buildings is improved or compromised in order to give the greatest benefit to the development as a whole. The intrusion of the motor car is controlled by lowering the visual dominance of car access and attempting to accommodate parking within the curtilage of the dwelling. Most buildings will be faced in render, though carefully selected and strategic buildings and facades have been executed in stone to maximise their visual impact.

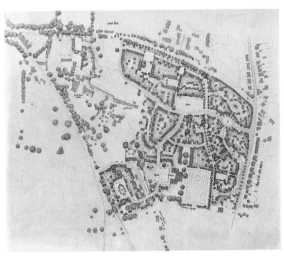

ABOVE: DRAWING OF VAGG STREET; *BELOW*: SITE PLAN

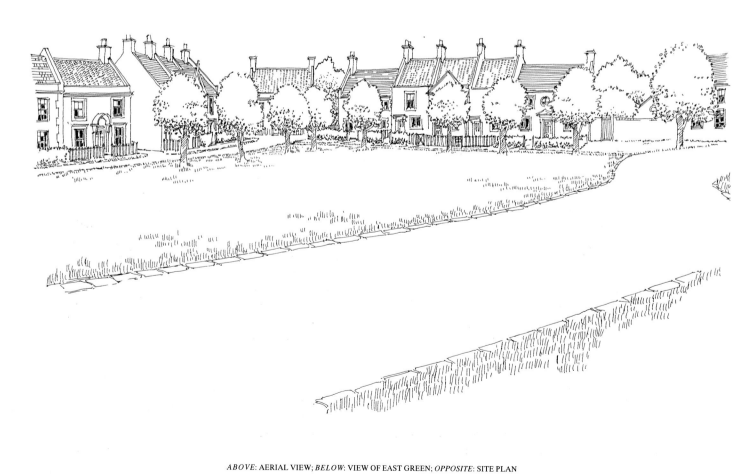

ABOVE: AERIAL VIEW; *BELOW*: VIEW OF EAST GREEN; *OPPOSITE*: SITE PLAN

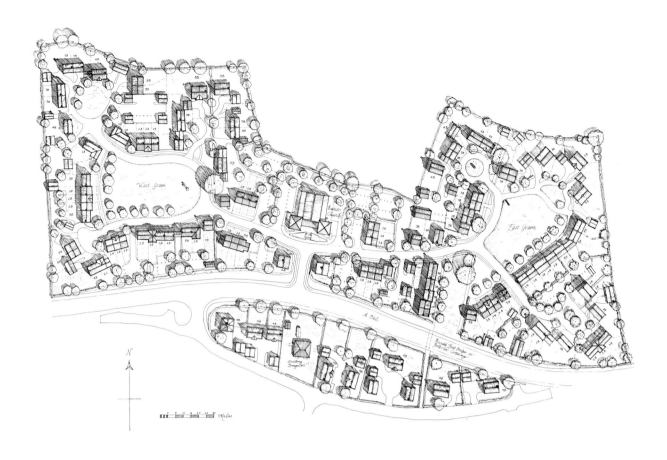

NEW HOUSING IN A VILLAGE PLAN
Midsomer Norton

A strip of agricultural land owned by the Duchy of Cornwall was scheduled as appropriate for development by Wansdyke District Council as a consequence of plans for the improvement of the A326 on the northern boundary of Midsomer Norton, a former coal mining town in Somerset. The site is of an awkward shape, the principal development area resembling a dumb-bell in plan. Midsomer Norton is not a large town and, although this area is relatively isolated by the new road, there is easy pedestrian access to the centre. The land slopes, at times quite steeply, towards town. Entry to the land from the proposed improved road is limited by curvature and the proximity of the narrow centre part of the dumb-bell to major junctions.

Market research was undertaken and a demand for smaller houses was revealed but the existing stock of older houses and the relatively low price range of housing generally placed severe financial restrictions on development. The site would take only 110 dwellings and, when considered in relation to nearby shopping and the isolated nature of the site, it was ascertained that a local shop could not be supported.

The configuration of the site and the existing provision of local small industrial and commercial units in the area made commercial uses impractical. A local church was interested in relocating and this gave the opportunity to provide a focal public building in the masterplan.

The public building is located in the narrow neck of the site, immediately opposite the point of access and on high ground above it. This will give a strong identity to the new development. From this point a spine road divides the access leading to two separate areas at each end of the dumb-bell. These two areas have been designed to group around two public spaces. Each space is of different design, to some degree dictated by the differing configuration of the areas and existing field boundaries. Although the vast majority of the housing consists of small dwellings, often arranged in terraces, some larger houses, generally on high ground, have been included to create a social and visual mix. The necessary passage of vehicles across or to the side of these public spaces is controlled by an informal treatment of the road surfaces in relation to the open area. Cars generally have access to dwellings from the rear, with the fronts facing onto public spaces. The conventional front to back relationship will therefore be modified by this arrangement.

The buildings are to be of simple design and executed in a limited range of traditional local materials. In practice this limits the roofing materials to pantile and slate and – due to the low market price of the buildings – the walls will be of render rather than local stone.

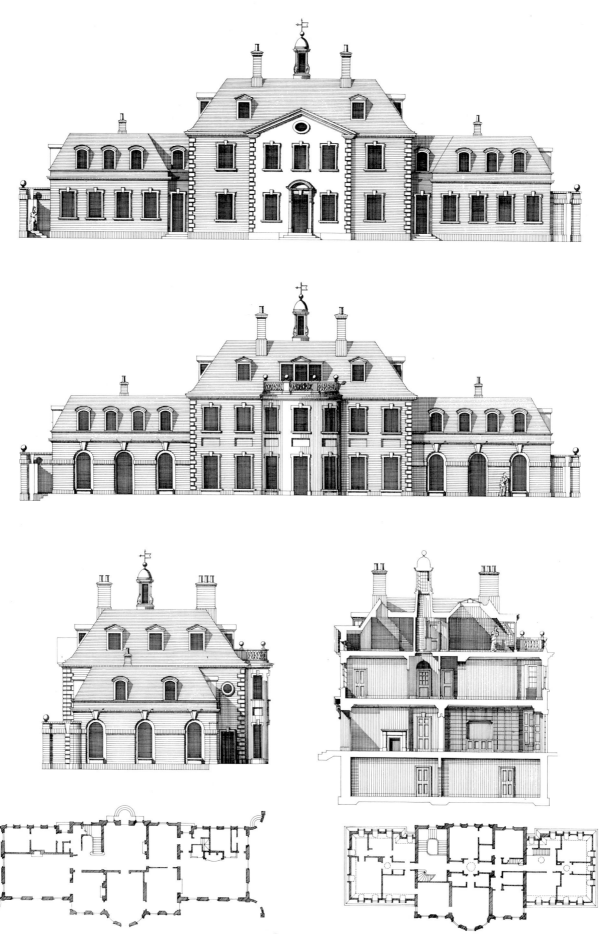

ABOVE: ELEVATIONS OF NORTH AND SOUTH FRONT; *ABOVE AND BELOW LEFT:* WEST FRONT AND GROUND FLOOR PLAN;
ABOVE AND BELOW RIGHT: SHORT SECTION AND SECOND FLOOR PLAN

JULIAN BICKNELL
UPTON VIVA
Warwickshire

Upton Viva enjoys extensive views over a traditional English landscape with the best prospects to the south. On the north side, the house and outbuilding shelter an entrance court from which the most spectacular views are hidden. Inside, the house has a formal (adult) wing to the west and an informal (children's) wing to the east. All the living rooms and most of the bedrooms on the floors above, look south over the landscape. The house also accommodates the estate offices.

ABOVE: BRACKETED DOORWAY; *BELOW*: GARDEN FACADE

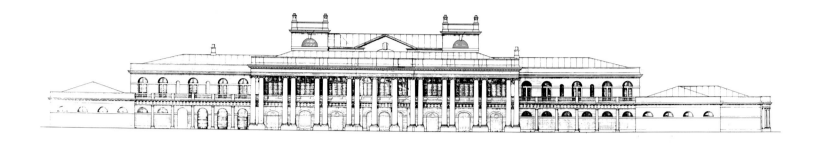

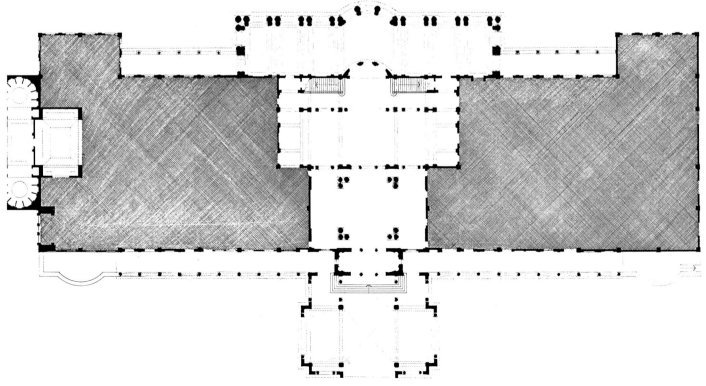

ABOVE: REAR ELEVATION; *CENTRE*: FRONT ELEVATION; *BELOW*: GROUND FLOOR PLAN

NAGARA COUNTRY CLUB
Japan

The Golf Club House for the Nagara Country Club, 30 miles from Tokyo serves as a gateway between the natural landscape of the forested hills of Chiba and the idealised landscape of the golf course. The English traditions of picturesque landscape design, with a serpentine approach road offering partly concealed glimpses of the building and the use of informal masses of trees and areas of water to enhance the natural forms of the landscape, suit the delicate social and sporting interactions of the Japanese golfing party. The ground floor of the building orders the approach to the course, with a magnificent entrance hall, flanked by changing rooms and service facilities. A large restaurant, private dining rooms and a VIP suite occupy the upper floor, with most rooms looking out over the golf course. The building will be opened in the spring of 1994.

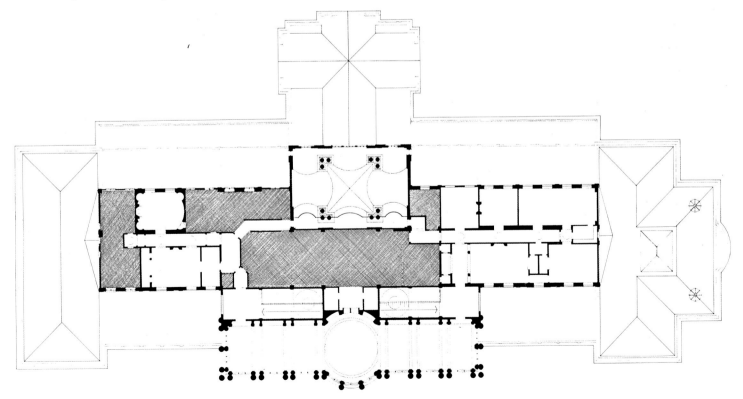

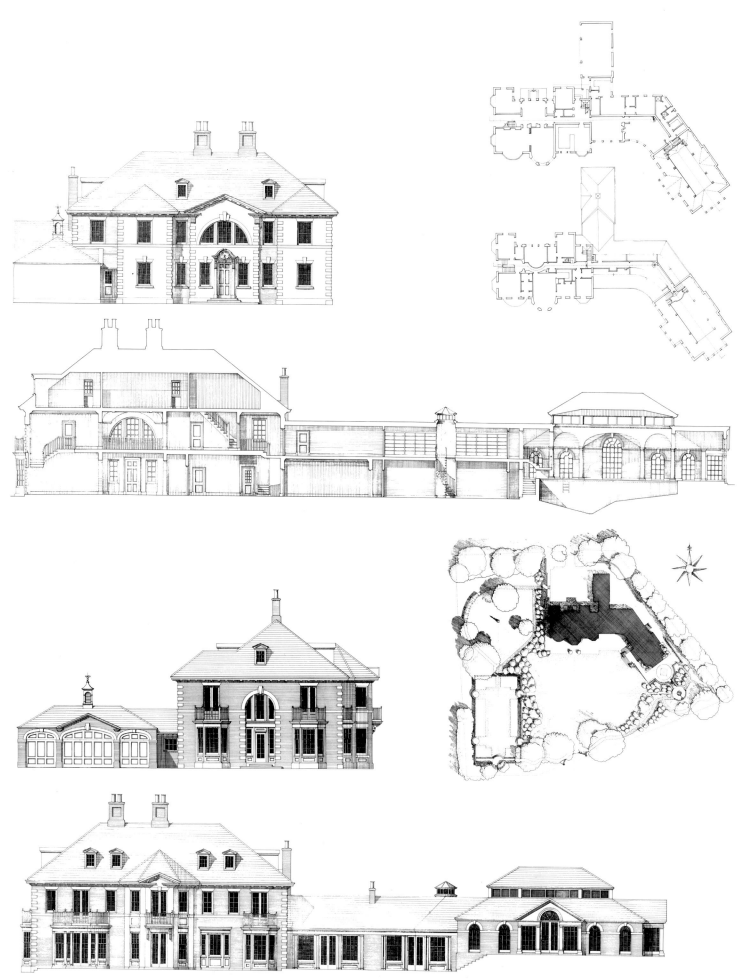

FROM ABOVE, LEFT TO RIGHT: ENTRANCE FACADE; GROUND AND FIRST FLOOR PLANS; LONGITUDINAL SECTION; WEST ELEVATION; SITE PLAN; GARDEN ELEVATION

HIGH CORNER
Surrey

In the tradition of the country house and its landscape two types have evolved. The first is the ideal, the isolated pavilion in an undifferentiated landscape surrounding the building on all sides; the other is more responsive to the exigencies of use, to access and orientation, and has an entrance side and a garden side, with different landscapes front and back.

High Corner is of the latter type. It faces south and west over a relatively small site, in an enclave of private houses on *the edge of the London conurbation, enjoying a boundary of mature trees and a view over grazing land beyond. The entrance court on the north side is enclosed with a garage building and high hedges so that the garden is only accessible through the house. All the living rooms look onto the garden, the formal living rooms and bedrooms occupying the west end of the house, the informal living rooms extending to a split level swimming pool to the east.*

ABOVE: BRACKETED DOORWAY; *BELOW*: ENTRANCE FACADE; *OVERLEAF*: VIEW FROM GARDEN

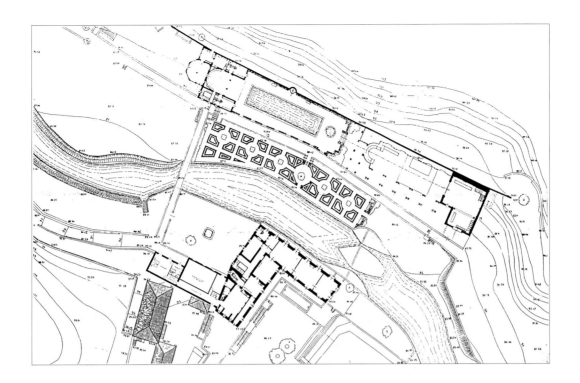

PIERRE BARBE
HOUSE AND FARM
Portugal

This estate, bought by Pierre Schlumberger in 1964 at Quinta Do Vinagre, was laid out by Pierre Barbe during the course of ten years between 1965 and 1975, during which time the main buildings were ravaged by a fire and the owner decided neither to continue the work nor to remain at La Quinta.

A river runs through the property. In 1968 Barbe entirely renovated the farmhouse opposite the main residence (which is an 18th-century building). He created two large terraces, one at a lower level leading onto a box hedge garden, and the other higher up on which stands a pavilion with a swimming-pool next to it and a house to be used for receptions. In 1973 Pierre Schlumberger asked Barbe to add a wing to the 18th-century house. This wing is completely harmonious with the rest of the building and indeed the less well-trained eye would have difficulty in telling where the old stops and the new begins.

From 1971 to 1975, Schlumberger undertook the construction of a model farm (a Marie-Antoinette style dairy). A bucolic utopia, this scheme allowed Barbe to design a powerful building close to the reveries of Ledoux, which would be a logical adjunct to the picturesque quality of the main house and its surroundings. Barbe has used two columns topped with simple Tuscan capitals for the swimming pool pavilion. This was a fantasy which he allowed himself since the columns were needed to frame a unique view of the banks of the Vinagre.

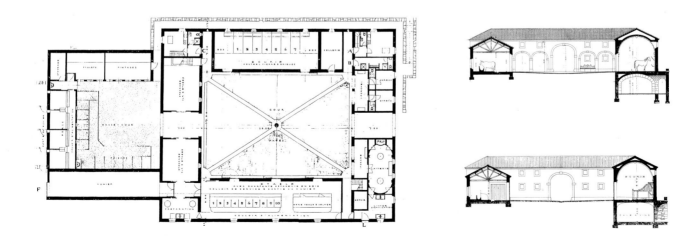

ABOVE: SITE PLAN OF HOUSE AND GARDEN; *BELOW*: FLOOR PLAN AND TRANSVERSAL SECTIONS OF FARM

ABOVE: GENERAL PLAN AND SECTION, SOUTH ELEVATION

PHILIPPE ROTTHIER
CAN GERXO
Ibiza

The client, who has lived on the island a long time, bought a hectare of agricultural land at the centre of a new building area: on this plot, on the south side of the slope were the ruins of a farmhouse.

There were two aims here: to restore the ancient stone walls, eroded by humidity and sea salt and then to reinstate the house as it originally was, by playing the archaeologist. Unwanted sections of wall were knocked down and those parts of the building which had been destroyed were reinvented. The reconstructed house covers exactly the same area as the original. In front of the porch a towering column with a

wooden cross beam is the symbolic feature of the house: this image, borrowed from a 19th-century engraving, was what sealed the contract between Frank and his architect.

The ancient character of the grounds has also been restored – terraces with support walls built on the original ones, a reservoir and an irrigation channel with a garage and threshing floor at the back of the house. At the sides two former corrals have been turned into a small studio annexe, with, in the foreground, a long horizontal chassis acting as a sunscreen – this is where Frank lived while the house was being built, which was done with him to the rhythm of the lunar calendar.

ABOVE: PORTICO; *BELOW*: VIEW OF SOUTH-WEST SIDE; *OVERLEAF*: VIEW OF SOUTH FACADE, PORCH AND INDEPENDENT STUDIO

ABOVE: VIEW OF SOUTH FACING PORCH AND TERRACE; *BELOW*: EAST FACADE

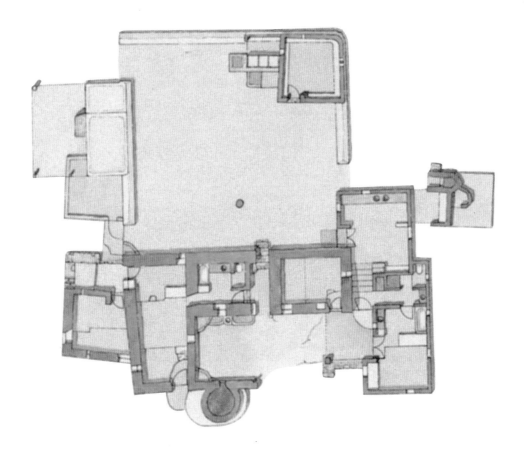

SA PAÏSSA DE'N CASETES
Ibiza

This is not a show house as is often the case with architects' homes. If there is a professional credence then it is a way of life, a way of building; step by step. Originally there was a small abandoned farmhouse. Gradually, the house grew bigger: two solid new living quarters were added on top of the old païssa, followed by a completely new and higher lateral addition, which was soon enhanced by a two-storey porch to create a balanced relationship between the old and the new.

Built by the architect and a few friends, the house was a test ground for technical and aesthetic solutions. Each stage was a new experience. New types of stonework were experimented with – stone, 'cyclopean' concrete and breezeblock – and a new form of lighting invented.

Further north, the cases noves group together to form a small house for some friends and the office of Taller d'Estudis de L'Habitat Pitius – a research and development agency set up by Philippe Rotthier in 1985. The workshops are for architecture and astrology. The construction of these were governed by the same logic and rhythm as the first.

The friends' house has been influenced by the American 'do-it-yourself' movement: a glass polyhedron, a troglodytic bathroom, a bed hanging from the roof and at the back two twin cubic workshops which make up the two basic cells of the traditional house in addition to the office of THEP.

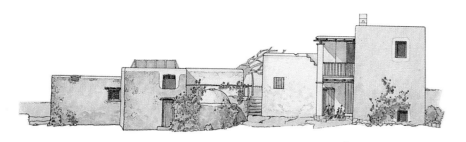

ABOVE: ELEVATION; *BELOW*: SOUTH ELEVATION

ABOVE: AERIAL VIEW OF GASSIN; *BELOW*: STREET SCENE

FRANÇOIS SPOERRY
VILLAGE DE GASSIN
France

The village of Gassin is situated high in the hills of the Saint Tropez peninsula. It is characterised by winding streets and paved squares which provide vistas over the surrounding landscape.

The project is an extension of the south side of the village and consists of apartments, shops, a fire station and a school, all built in the character of the region.

The project's aim is to bring life back into the village and secure its economic future by providing a mix of functions, a dialogue between public and private space and respect for the integrity of the countryside. The extension of the village was commissioned by the local authority and has been built exclusively for the local population in traditional materials.

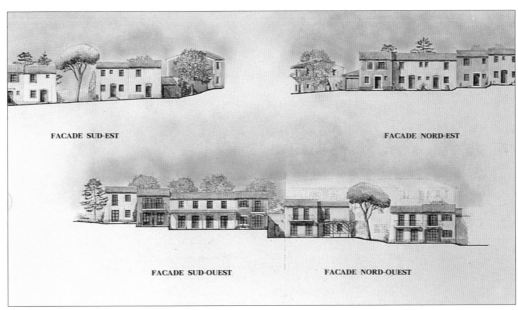

ABOVE: VIEW OF THE MODEL; *BELOW*: THE FACADES

HOUSES IN GASSIN